HEALTH REPORTS:
DISEASES AND DISORDERS

ADHD

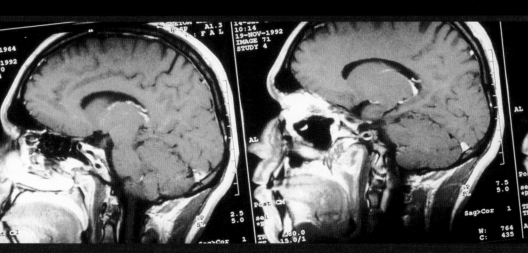

AMY FARRAR

TWENTY-FIRST CENTURY BOOKS
MINNEAPOLIS

Twenty-First Century Books
A division of Lerner Publishing Group, Inc.
241 First Avenue North
Minneapolis, MN 55401 U.S.A.

Website address: www.lernerbooks.com

Library of Congress Cataloging-in-Publication Data

Farrar, Amy.
    ADHD / by Amy Farrar.
        p.   cm. — (USA Today health reports: Diseases and disorders)
    Includes bibliographical references and index.
        ISBN 978–0–7613–5455–0 (lib. bdg. : alk. paper)
        1. Attention-deficit hyperactivity disorder—Popular works. I. Title.
    II. Title: Attention deficit disorder and Attention deficit hyperactivity disorder.
    RJ506.H9F37 2011
    618.92'8589—dc22   2010000870

Manufactured in the United States of America
1 – DP – 7/15/10

CONTENTS

USA TODAY
HEALTH REPORTS:
DISEASES AND DISORDERS

WHAT IS ADHD?

My son never sits still for a minute. He can't focus on anything. If I don't sit with him, he doesn't do his homework. And when he does do it, he forgets to turn it in. He is so smart. But unless he's doing something that doesn't bore him, like his video games, he has trouble focusing. He interrupts constantly and never finishes what he starts.

Does this describe you? Does it describe someone you know or love? Then you (or that person) might have attention deficit hyperactivity disorder (ADHD). ADHD is a neurobehavioral disorder, a disorder of the nervous system that can be seen in a person's behavior. People with ADHD have difficulty paying attention. They often cannot focus on specific tasks. Some people with ADHD are also hyperactive (more active than is usual) and can be impulsive—they do things without thinking them through.

Some people don't think ADHD is a real medical problem. Or they think ADHD is just a term people use when they can't explain another person's behavior. Some people even joke that they're "having an ADHD moment" when they can't find something, such as a cell phone. It's hard for people without ADHD to understand the difference between ADHD symptoms and daydreaming and forgetfulness. Some people think doctors are too quick to diagnose ADHD. On the other hand, many doctors say too many people with ADHD are never treated because it isn't diagnosed enough.

Most people with ADHD are children, so some people blame the symptoms on bad parenting. Some people say that watching too much television or playing too many video games can cause ADHD. This may contribute to ADHD, but in most cases, people

News
SECTION A

April 5, 2004

From the Pages of USA TODAY

Short attention span linked to TV

The link between watching television and attention problems has concerned doctors and parents for a long time. The American Academy of Pediatrics says kids older than two should watch no more than two hours of television per day. The academy says that children younger than two shouldn't watch any television at all, and television programs for older kids should be educational and right for their age.

Dimitri Christakis, a pediatrician at Children's Hospital and Regional Medical Center in Seattle [Washington], used a government database to see how much television one- to three-year-old children watched. Information in the database had been collected by the children's mothers.

After reviewing the data, Christakis then compared it to scores from a behavior checklist showing attention problems at age seven that were gathered on about 1,300 kids.

The research showed that children who watch a lot of TV in early childhood are the most likely to have concentration problems, impulsiveness, and restlessness. Not all of these children had ADHD, but many did have it, and the others were at risk for major learning problems.

The research also showed that every added hour of watching TV increases a child's odds of having attention problems by about 10 percent!

—*Marilyn Elias*

with ADHD have a chemical imbalance—their brains don't have the right amounts of certain chemicals.

ADHD is a very real problem that involves a lot more than just forgetting where you put your cell phone or zoning out in front of the television. Doctors and researchers were recording these types of behaviors long before they knew what to call the disorder.

There are three types of ADHD: inattentive (lacking attention), hyperactive/impulsive, and a combination of both inattentive and

ADHD or ADD?

Over the years, attention deficit hyperactivity disorder has had several other names, including attention deficit disorder (ADD). In 1994 the American Psychiatric Association officially changed the name from ADD to ADHD. After that date, a person who would have been diagnosed with ADD in the past was identified as having inattentive type ADHD. Essentially, this is ADHD with very little or no hyperactivity.

hyperactive/impulsive. Most people have either the inattentive or combined type. Some people have ADHD that is in partial remission—many of the symptoms no longer present a problem for them. Remission often occurs as people age. Others have ADHD that is "otherwise not specified"—their symptoms do not fit into the typical categories of ADHD.

Researchers say genes play a large role in whether a person will have ADHD or not. Genes are biological units people inherit from their parents and ancestors that determine things like eye and hair color and the possibility of developing certain diseases. If a child has one or two parents who have ADHD, that child is very likely to also have ADHD.

HOW COMMON IS ADHD?

Medical professionals use the word *prevalence* to describe the number of individuals in a population who are affected by a disease or disorder at a given time. Since the disorder was defined by the

American Psychiatric Association in 1994, a number of studies have investigated the prevalence of ADHD. However, the identification of the disorder is relatively new and different organizations have come up with various results. The National Institute of Mental Health (NIMH) estimates that about 2 million children in the United States have ADHD. That's between 3 and 5 percent of children in the United States, which means in a class of twenty-five to thirty students, at least one student will have ADHD. In 2003 the Centers for Disease Control and Prevention (CDC) reported that about 4.4 million children between the ages of four and seventeen were diagnosed with ADHD.

In a typical classroom of twenty-five to thirty students, at least one student is likely to have ADHD.

And according to the Attention Deficit Disorder Association, ADHD affects 6 to 10 percent of children and 3 to 6 percent of adults in the United States.

One thing that most researchers agree on is that males are affected more often than females. Many girls with the disorder are never diagnosed because girls are less likely to be hyperactive. Since they mostly have the inattentive type of ADHD, these girls are often seen by others as being spacey or unintelligent.

At one time, ADHD was thought to go away after adolescence. But the American Academy of Child and Adolescent Psychiatry views ADHD as a chronic, or ongoing, condition that continues into adulthood about half the time. Some researchers believe that more than 50 percent of people with ADHD continue to suffer as adults.

Researchers are finding that ADHD often extends into adulthood. And more adults are identifying their difficulty concentrating and occasional quick temper as symptoms of ADHD.

Many adults with the disorder were not diagnosed as children because doctors and parents didn't know about ADHD. Adults with ADHD have difficulty concentrating and may have trouble controlling anger.

Researchers continue to try to understand the causes of ADHD and develop effective treatments. An important point to remember is that early diagnosis and treatment are crucial. People with ADHD who do not receive treatment may experience failure at school, depression and other psychological disorders, failed relationships and careers, and substance abuse. People with ADHD can lead normal, satisfying lives if they receive early, appropriate treatment.

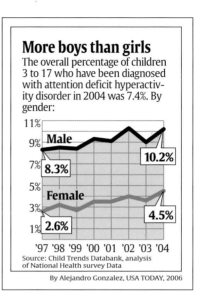

More boys than girls

The overall percentage of children 3 to 17 who have been diagnosed with attention deficit hyperactivity disorder in 2004 was 7.4%. By gender:

Male — 8.3% ... 10.2%
Female — 2.6% ... 4.5%

'97 '98 '99 '00 '01 '02 '03 '04

Source: Child Trends Databank, analysis of National Health survey Data

By Alejandro Gonzalez, USA TODAY, 2006

CHAPTER ONE

ADHD THEN AND NOW

Katie Jo is a bright, energetic thirteen-year-old girl who has a passion for animals and loves to barrel race with her horse (she also teaches cardiopulmonary resuscitation—to adults!). Katie Jo's mother, Debi, describes her as "very animated and alive. She has lots of friends and she is very active in school."

ADHD was part of Katie Jo's family history. Her brothers have some version of the disorder. Her oldest brother, Steven, was never formally diagnosed, and her brother Tim had hyperactivity. He was destructive and angry. When Tim was young, Debi didn't know much about ADHD and never put Tim on medications. She tried dietary changes, such as limiting how much sugar he ate. But the changes didn't help. Despite a lot of setbacks, Tim became a successful carpenter. Tim feels he leads a good life, despite not being treated for ADHD. Katie Jo's brother Daniel was diagnosed with mild ADD and dysgraphia when he turned fifteen. (Dysgraphia is a disorder that makes it difficult to write, even if someone has normal reading and thinking skills.) "I felt I was a failure as a parent," says Debi. "I was challenged with a lot of things. I was a single parent raising my kids on my own, so every day was a challenge. I struggled hard with trying to do the right thing."

ADHD THROUGH HISTORY

In 1844 a German doctor named Heinrich Hoffmann described the symptoms of ADHD. *Struwwelpeter (Slovenly Peter)*, a book of stories in verse Hoffmann wrote for his three-year-old son Carl Philip, told the story of Fidgety Philip, a child who could not sit through a meal and fidgeted until he fell out of his chair. The story opens:

Let me see if Philip can
Be a little gentleman;
Let me see, if he is able
To sit still for once at table:
Thus Papa bade Phil behave;
And Mamma look'd very grave.
But fidgety Phil,
He won't sit still;
He wriggles
And giggles,
And then, I declare,
Swings backwards and forwards
And tilts up his chair,
Just like any rocking horse; —
"Philip! I am getting cross!"

This 1847 illustration shows a character named Philip fidgeting at the supper table. In the 1844 book *Struwwelpeter* (Slovenly Peter) the author, Heinrich Hoffmann, describes Philip, who displays many of the symptoms of ADHD.

The story goes on to describe how Philip's fidgeting causes him to fall backward in his chair. As he falls, he takes the tablecloth with him, sending everything on the table crashing to the floor. In the end, his parents can't find him because he's covered with the tablecloth and dishes.

About six years later, British pediatrician George Still described ADHD. Dr. Still studied forty-three children who had short attention spans. The children were aggressive, frequently challenging others verbally or physically. They were also defiant—they argued with

At the end of Philip's story, he takes the contents of the table with him as he crashes to the floor. Like Philip, children with ADHD don't always foresee the consequences of their actions.

everyone and did not respect authority. Dr. Still described these children as having a lack of moral control, meaning he believed they couldn't control themselves. Still believed there was a biological (physical) reason for this behavior. He also noted that people with ADHD often have tic disorders. A tic is a twitch or other movement a person can't control, often occurring in the face. Dr. Still believed that "normal behavior" in children was defined by comparing them to their peers and not by comparing them to younger or older children.

From 1917 to 1918, the world faced two major public health crises: a widespread outbreak of encephalitis (swelling of the brain caused by a virus) and an influenza pandemic (a widespread outbreak of flu). Some of the children who survived these outbreaks had similar behavioral problems to those found in children with ADHD. Doctors described them as having "minimal brain damage." Then experts believed that this minimal brain damage caused ADHD. The idea of minimal brain damage as a cause of ADHD eventually disappeared because there was no real scientific evidence to prove that people with ADHD had brain damage.

In the 1950s and 1960s, experts introduced the terms *hyperactive child syndrome*, *hyperkinetic syndrome*, and *hyperkinetic reaction of childhood* to describe ADHD. Hyperkinesia is an abnormal increase in muscular activity that people often cannot control. Researchers thought that the brains of people with ADHD couldn't process stimulation, such as light, sounds, words, and pictures. The researchers never completely proved their theory. But their research was important because it was the first time anyone had sought a more specific reason for hyperactivity.

Katie Jo was diagnosed with ADD (without hyperactivity or any other conditions) in third grade. Before Katie Jo was diagnosed, she struggled a lot. At home and at school, Katie Jo was forgetful and easily distracted, and she couldn't focus or pay attention. She had trouble concentrating in school and doing her homework. She was disorganized, and her grades suffered. Katie Jo had to repeat third grade.

Katie Jo's pediatrician sent her to an ADHD testing center, where a nurse practitioner diagnosed her with ADHD without hyperactivity. Soon Katie Jo was taking a drug called Ritalin twice a day. Within four months, she was getting As on her spelling tests, turning in her homework, and was at the top of her math and reading classes. Katie Jo says it felt good to understand what she was doing and to be able to remember what she had read.

Katie Jo had always thought that her teachers and other school staff didn't like her because she was disruptive in class. And at first, she was embarrassed by her diagnosis because she had to go to the school office to take her medications. But once her medications began to work and the school nurse and her teachers began telling her what a great job she was doing in school and how proud they all were of her, she started to realize that being treated for ADD was a good thing. It was a new experience for her to be the teacher's pet, and it made her feel good when her teachers from previous years made a point of talking to her.

According to Debi, people notice when Katie Jo isn't taking her medication, "because she doesn't think right. She does things she wouldn't normally do." Debi says behavioral counseling helped Katie Jo a lot.

VIEWS AND RESEARCH

During this time, ideas about ADHD in the United States differed from views in Europe, especially in Great Britain. Experts in the United States saw hyperactivity as a fairly common behavioral disorder. But British researchers believed it was connected to some kind of brain damage, trauma, or infection. As a result, diagnosis and treatment for ADHD in these two countries was very different.

In the 1970s, researchers began to look more closely at the inattentive type of ADHD. Possible causes for ADHD were said to include diet and environment. Many people blamed technology and fast-paced lifestyles for higher rates of hyperactivity in children. Research started to focus on the effects of stimulant medications on school-age children with ADHD. Stimulants increase brain activity, alertness, attention, and energy. They also raise blood pressure and increase the heart rate and breathing rate. The research showed that stimulants were an effective treatment for ADHD. This research resulted in a rapid increase in their use.

In 1975 the U.S. Congress passed Public Law 94-142, or the Individuals with Disabilities Education Act (IDEA). To receive federal funds, states must create and put into effect policies that ensure a free and appropriate public education for children with disabilities. To qualify for services under IDEA, a student with ADHD must have one of thirteen conditions outlined in the law.

In the 1980s, the American Psychiatric Association (APA) developed more specific guidelines for diagnosing ADHD. In 1987 the APA changed the disorder's name from ADD to ADHD. Researchers began looking at what role society plays in ADHD. They wanted to know how environment and relationships with peers, teachers, parents, and family members could affect ADHD. The APA developed rating scales to help doctors diagnose ADHD. Research continued on the effects of medications used to treat ADHD. In the 1990s, medical professionals identified the three main ADHD types: inattentive, hyperactive, and combined.

Doctors have made many advances in treatment since the 1980s. Most doctors and therapists agree that the best approach is a combination of education about the disorder, behavioral therapy, and medication. They also agree that every person with ADHD has different needs. Many organizations for individuals with ADHD and their families have sprung up in recent years. Most of these organizations seek to educate people with ADHD, their families, and the general public.

In fourth grade, Katie Jo's medication didn't seem to work as well for her. As she describes it, "The medication made me really angry." So Debi took Katie Jo to a psychologist, who switched the medication to Concerta. Debi says the Concerta helps Katie Jo a lot. But so does Katie Jo's awareness of her disorder. She knows when ADHD is affecting her and what to do about it. Katie Jo does not take medication on weekends or during the summer, when concentration isn't as important as it is when she's in school. Debi says that coping with ADHD in the family became easier once she understood that it is "truly an illness and not a behavior problem."

MYTHS ABOUT ADHD

Despite increasing knowledge about ADHD, many people still do not understand that it is a serious disorder. Some people think that ADHD in children is caused by bad parenting. They think that parents don't discipline their children and that children are just "acting out" to get attention. This viewpoint makes an already difficult situation even harder for kids with ADHD and their parents. Most parents of children with ADHD want to help their kids, but they need the right information to do so. One study conducted by the National Institute of Mental Health (NIMH) showed that parents who developed a disciplined yet positive approach to managing their child's symptoms noted improved behavior over time.

May 25, 2005

From the Pages of USA TODAY

Teen girls with ADHD at higher risk of mental illness; early treatment vital, study finds

Attention deficit/hyperactivity disorder (ADHD) is a serious problem for teenage girls, and those who have it appear to be at much higher risk for mental illness by age 17, a Harvard Medical School researcher reported.

The largest, most thorough study so far comparing girls with ADHD with peers who don't have it underscores the importance of early diagnosis and treatment, says study leader Joseph Biederman, a child psychiatrist. He spoke at the American Psychiatric Association meeting.

Biederman's study tracked 140 girls with ADHD from ages 12 to 17 and compared them with 122 girls without the disorder. By 17, the ADHD girls were far more likely to be clinically depressed, to have anxiety disorders, and to have conduct disorder.

About ten boys are referred for ADHD treatment for every girl "and 99 percent of the childhood ADHD research is on boys," Biederman says. He believes it's because girls don't become disruptive as early in life as boys with ADHD do, so it often goes undiagnosed.

Among other ADHD reports presented at the meeting:

- Scientists are zeroing in on genes linked to ADHD, Harvard neuroscientist Pamela Sklar says. Genetics accounts for about 76 percent of a person's odds of developing the disorder.
- Small brain-scan studies in adults seem to confirm larger studies in kids showing that the brains of those with ADHD look different than those who don't have it, reports Harvard neuropsychologist Larry Seidman.

"We know it's a disorder that goes on across the life span and is brain-based," says Peg Nichols of Children and Adults with Attention Deficit/Hyperactivity Disorder, an advocacy group.

But the usefulness of genetic and high-tech studies is questionable, says Walnut Creek, California behavioral pediatrician Lawrence Diller.

"Behavior can change the brain—it goes in both directions," he says. "And there's a lot of misdiagnosis out there. Many kids in studies are quite impaired, not like the Tom Sawyers and Pippi Longstockings brought to my office for ADHD workups."

—Marilyn Elias

People still believe the multitude of myths about ADHD. The most prevalent one is that it is caused by bad parenting. The fact is that the causes of ADHD aren't known, but are likely a complicated combination of chemical, environmental, and genetic factors.

Other people blame the symptoms of ADHD on diet, laziness, the environment (pollution, electronics, etc.), a bad attitude, and other factors. While all of these things may make ADHD worse, they do not cause it.

Some doctors say that too many people are said to have the disorder, and some of them may not truly have it. Doctors sometimes diagnose people incorrectly. When this happens, people without ADHD take unneeded medications or people who really do have the disorder go without medications and other treatments that could be helpful.

One theory about ADHD is that people with the disorder can use it to their advantage. For example, some people think that people with ADHD make great soldiers, doctors, ambulance drivers, firefighters, and 9-1-1 operators; in short, any job in which they have to be extremely focused or quickly switch their attention from one thing to another. There certainly are many people with ADHD who have successful careers, but this theory downplays the seriousness of the disorder.

The important thing to remember is that people with ADHD can lead productive lives and can attain their dreams, but they need to find out what the best treatment and coping methods for them are. The more people with ADHD know about the disorder, the more successful they will be in life. They need to be able to make good choices about their personal and professional lives. People with ADHD or their parents must also make sure that everybody around them (teachers, doctors, and employers) has the information they need to provide the right kind of support.

CHAPTER TWO

SYMPTOMS AND CAUSES OF ADHD

Calvin is a very smart eight-year-old boy. Like a lot of other boys his age, Calvin loves to play video games and basketball. Calvin's mother, Rebecca, says that to many people, "he appears a little quirky and highly energetic." Anyone who spends more time with Calvin, however, notices that he constantly fidgets, always moving some part of his body.

Rebecca says Calvin was fairly mellow as a baby. But when he turned two and a half, he started showing some unusual behaviors, including violent tantrums and rages that no one could explain. He would also walk on the tips of his toes and flap his hands. Rebecca and her husband, Dennis, could not bring Calvin with them when they went on family outings. Then one of Calvin's preschool teachers noted that Calvin was having trouble interacting with his peers.

SYMPTOMS OF ADHD

ADHD symptoms usually begin in childhood before the age of seven and can vary depending on the type of ADHD. Inattention, hyperactivity, and impulsivity are the main behaviors found in people with ADHD. According to the NIMH, all children have these behaviors at times. But these behaviors are more severe and happen more often in children with ADHD.

Symptoms of inattention can include the following:
- Being easily distracted, missing details, forgetting things, and frequently switching from one activity to another
- Having difficulty focusing on tasks or play
- Becoming bored with a task after only a few minutes if it isn't enjoyable

- Having difficulty organizing tasks or activities or learning something new
- Having trouble completing tasks or following through (for example, turning in homework assignments)
- Often losing things (pencils, toys, and assignments) needed to complete tasks or activities
- Avoiding tasks that require sustained (unbroken) attention
- Appearing to not listen when spoken to
- Daydreaming, becoming easily confused, and moving slowly
- Having difficulty processing information as quickly and accurately as others
- Struggling to follow instructions

People with ADHD often look distracted and do not appear to be paying attention, even when spoken to.

Symptoms of hyperactivity may include:

- Fidgeting and squirming while sitting or not being able to sit still at all
- Talking nonstop
- Dashing around, touching or playing with anything and everything in sight
- Not being able to stay seated
- Being constantly in motion
- Having difficulty doing quiet tasks or activities

Symptoms of impulsivity may include:

- Being very impatient
- Blurting out inappropriate comments or talking out of turn
- Showing emotions without restraint
- Acting without being concerned about the action's consequences
- Having difficulty waiting for things or waiting for turns in games
- Interrupting conversations or others' activities

Hyperactivity is one of the most obvious symptoms of ADHD.

Impulsivity can cause people with ADHD to start arguments for no apparent reason or to blurt things out without fear of the consequences.

Not everyone with ADHD has all of these symptoms. For someone to be diagnosed with ADHD, he or she must have had symptoms for six months or more. In children, the symptoms must be greater than similar behaviors observed in other children of the same age. To confirm a specific ADHD type, a person must have a specific number of signs and symptoms.

Most people with ADHD have a hard time focusing on activities they find boring, such as cleaning, planning, and doing homework. Most of them don't have a problem focusing on activities they find really interesting or exciting. This trait can be a good thing if they focus on something they want to achieve and it doesn't interfere with other responsibilities. But focusing too much on the wrong things can have a negative effect. For example, a boy who plays video games for hours on end can completely lose track of the time and ignore his schoolwork and chores. Although everyone, including people without ADHD, can fall into these patterns, this struggle is greatly exaggerated for a lot of people with ADHD.

Many children with ADHD have difficulty switching from one activity to another. They may complain about having to move on to something else, physically resist their parents by refusing to move, scream and shout, or whine. They may have problems in new environments and may throw tantrums or show other negative

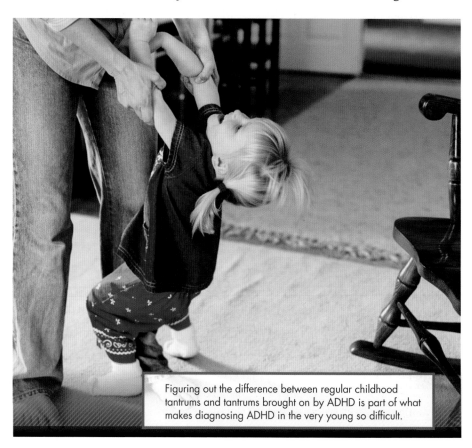

Figuring out the difference between regular childhood tantrums and tantrums brought on by ADHD is part of what makes diagnosing ADHD in the very young so difficult.

behaviors in unfamiliar places, especially if there is a lot of noise and activity.

ADHD affects the brain's higher thought processes that help with planning and problem solving. These thought processes also help people learn from the past, think before they make decisions, and reach goals. When these thought processes do not work properly, as in many people with ADHD, it can be very difficult to reach goals.

People with ADHD can have a hard time making and keeping friends because they misread social cues, which can make their interactions with others very awkward. Adults with ADHD may be lonely and isolated because they never learned basic social skills, such as listening without interrupting, being polite, and following through on plans and responsibilities.

One of the most difficult problems they develop is poor self-esteem. This can result from constantly receiving negative feedback and criticism from others. Self-esteem is also affected by repeated failure and the constant struggle to succeed. People with ADHD often feel that they are just stupid, lazy, slow, or incapable.

Hyperactivity in ADHD may go away or become less noticeable as children become young adults. This is one reason that doctors may not diagnose adults with ADHD, even though they may have other symptoms, such as difficulty staying on task.

Gifted children are sometimes incorrectly diagnosed with ADHD. Their curiosity, impatience, perfectionism, and intensity are qualities that are also common in children with ADHD. Gifted children may also be quick to challenge authority and they may be hyperactive. Sometimes children with ADHD are also gifted. This possible confusion is another reason children who are suspected of having ADHD should receive a thorough evaluation for the disorder by a qualified professional, so that they get the therapy and educational interventions they need to thrive and succeed.

www.usatoday.com

USA TODAY

Life
SECTION D

February 6, 1990

From the Pages of USA TODAY

Families struggle with kids' hyperactive behavior

Lynda Stauffer first noticed the change in her 7-year-old son Matthew last summer.

"We started (seeing) a lot of frustration in his behavior," she recalls. Matthew would write with crayon on the floor of his bedroom and the walls of the den. "And there would be angry outbursts—very juvenile behavior," she says.

When school started, things got worse. "He was really frustrating his teacher: talking in class, being very forgetful, not being able to follow orders," says Stauffer, 38, a substitute teacher in Simpsonville, S.C.

These episodes were the first indications that Matthew suffers from attention deficit hyperactivity disorder (ADHD), a condition affecting 3 percent to 5 percent of U.S. children. And Matthew's problems provide a typical example of how the disorder affects kids.

His behavior in class became disruptive, his mother says. "Matthew could not concentrate long enough to listen to instructions. And then he would be too embarrassed to ask the teacher to repeat

A family psychologist recommended that Rebecca and Dennis take Calvin to an occupational therapist. These trained professionals help people who are ill or disabled learn to manage everyday tasks, such as getting dressed and preparing meals. The occupational therapist diagnosed Calvin with sensory integrative dysfunction disorder (SID), which meant Calvin's brain had difficulty processing information from his five senses (sight, touch, hearing, taste, and smell). Although people with SID can use their five senses like other people, the sensory information can cause them stress or confusion. At the same time Calvin tested positive for SID, he also tested at borderline levels for ADHD, Asperger's syndrome (a mild form of autism), and autism.

it. So he would bother other students by acting like a class clown to try to get information, hiding his inability to concentrate."

In addition, Matthew's self-esteem sank to the point where any rebuke or correction from his teacher would make him feel terrible about himself, his mother says.

The teacher, understandably, was upset. "She just lamented about how Matthew was bothering her," Stauffer says.

Finally, in November, the Stauffers took Matthew to a psychologist for tests.

That's when they learned their son has ADHD, which is six to nine times more common in boys than in girls, says Dr. James Satterfield of the National Center for Hyperactive Children in Encino, Calif.

Its symptoms include extreme fidgetiness (can't sit still, fingers always tapping), distractibility (short attention span, easily diverted by things others ignore)

and impulsivity (they don't stop to think before they act), says child psychiatrist Dr. Larry B. Silver of Georgetown University School of Medicine in Washington, D.C.

Those with the condition may have one symptom, two or all three, Silver says.

A further complication: about half also have a learning disability, Satterfield says.

ADHD has nothing to do with intelligence. "Many of these kids have IQs that are in the superior range," he says.

The condition usually begins before age 6, and more often by age 2 or 3. While it sometimes disappears by late teens, one-third to two-thirds of the cases continue into adulthood, Satterfield says.

ADHD is often misdiagnosed. One reason: The same symptoms are more likely to have emotional causes such as anxiety or depression, Silver says. "The least-common cause is this neurological problem called ADHD," he says.

—Dan Sperling

Asperger's syndrome and autism are disorders that delay basic abilities. Children with autism have problems interacting and communicating with others and often cannot use their imaginations in pretend play. Children with Asperger's syndrome also have a hard time interacting and communicating. They may have average or above-average intelligence and normal language and thinking skills. But they may have a hard time concentrating and they may be clumsy.

Calvin took special education classes, including speech therapy, during preschool and kindergarten. He also took a social skills class that helped him learn how to interact with others. Calvin did so well in the class that he was able to attend regular classes when he entered first grade.

Calvin received his diagnosis of ADHD (combined type) when he was eight years old. His evaluation team included a medical doctor, a psychologist, two registered nurses, a speech specialist, and his primary care physician. They diagnosed him based on multiple tests, medical and educational records, and observations of his behavior, among other methods.

ADHD AND OTHER DISORDERS

People with ADHD often have other disorders in addition to ADHD. Many times these disorders overshadow their ADHD, so doctors do not diagnose ADHD as early as they might otherwise. These overlapping disorders can include:

- Learning disorders (can include difficulty learning a specific skill or subject, such as math or reading)
- Oppositional defiant disorder (ODD): continually fighting against authority figures and disobeying them beyond what is considered normal, arguing too much with others, annoying others on purpose, and blaming others for one's own mistakes. Approximately half of all children with the hyperactive/impulsive and combined types of ADHD also have ODD.
- Conduct disorder: antisocial behavior that can include stealing and bullying
- Asperger's syndrome and autism: disorders that affect thinking, feeling, language, and the ability to relate to others
- Sensory integrative dysfunction (SID) disorder: difficulty processing information from the five senses
- Bipolar disorder: a mood disorder that causes swings in mood from very happy to very sad and irritable
- Tourette's syndrome: a disorder of the nervous system that causes nervous tics

People with the hyperactive and/or impulsive type of ADHD are more likely to be injured than people without ADHD because they are so easily distracted. They are also more prone to substance abuse, using cigarettes, alcohol, or other drugs.

ADHD can also lead to anxiety, depression, and eating disorders. Girls with ADHD are more likely to dislike their bodies and be overweight. Girls with ADHD are also more at risk for bingeing (eating large amounts in a short period of time) or bingeing and purging (deliberately throwing up) when they become adolescents. They may have trouble getting along with peers and with parents, which makes their eating disorders worse. Boys with ADHD are also more likely to develop eating disorders than other boys.

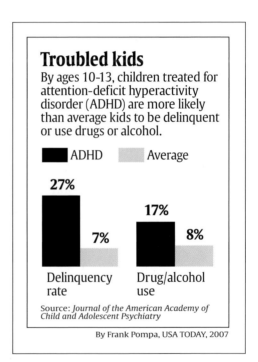

Troubled kids

By ages 10-13, children treated for attention-deficit hyperactivity disorder (ADHD) are more likely than average kids to be delinquent or use drugs or alcohol.

■ ADHD   ■ Average

27%
7%
Delinquency rate

17%
8%
Drug/alcohol use

Source: *Journal of the American Academy of Child and Adolescent Psychiatry*

By Frank Pompa, USA TODAY, 2007

CAUSES OF ADHD

According to the NIMH, no one knows for sure what causes ADHD. The levels of certain chemicals in the brain, genes, environmental factors such as poor nutrition, and combinations of all these things can contribute to ADHD.

THE BRAIN AND ADHD

People with ADHD usually have an imbalance of the chemicals dopamine and norepinephrine. Dopamine controls movement, emotion, motivation, and the feeling of pleasure. Low levels of dopamine have been proven to cause problems with inattention. Norepinephrine is a stress hormone (chemical in the body) that controls the body's "fight or flight" response. This is the brain's signal to the body to either fight or flee from a threat. Norepinephrine also plays a big role in attention and focus.

Many researchers say that the problem with ADHD isn't exactly attention. They believe that chemical imbalances in the brain make it impossible for people with these imbalances to make the connection between their behavior and the consequences that may result.

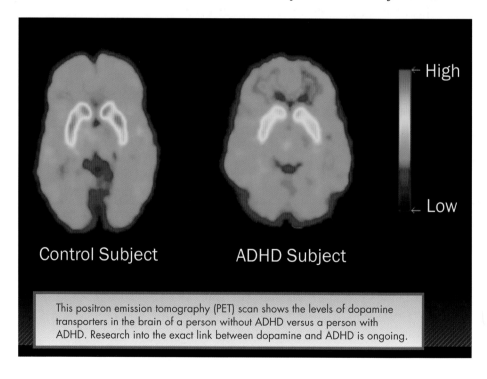

Control Subject   ADHD Subject

This positron emission tomography (PET) scan shows the levels of dopamine transporters in the brain of a person without ADHD versus a person with ADHD. Research into the exact link between dopamine and ADHD is ongoing.

Researchers have found that an area of the brain called the putamen is less active in children with ADHD. The amount of blood that flows to the putamen is less than normal in some children, which can lead to inattentiveness and hyperactivity.

Other researchers have found physical differences between the brains of children who have ADHD and those who do not. Some regions of the brain may develop more slowly. The delay the researchers identified was found most often at the front of the brain's outer section, called the cortex, which helps control thinking, attention, and planning.

GENES AND ADHD

Children whose parents have ADHD have a 50 percent (or greater) chance of developing ADHD. Several genes have been identified with ADHD. Genes are found within the cells of every living thing. They are the instruction manuals for our bodies, providing directions on how we look and function. A specific gene called *DRD47* may decrease levels of dopamine in the brain. People with ADHD are twice as likely to have this gene. Researchers are looking at how certain things might trigger symptoms in people who have this gene and others found in people with ADHD. For example, environmental factors such as living in a polluted area or being under stress might trigger symptoms.

OTHER POSSIBLE CAUSES OF ADHD

Many other factors might cause ADHD. Pregnant women who smoke, drink, or use drugs might put their babies at risk for developing ADHD. Alcohol or drug abuse during pregnancy may reduce activity of the nerve cells that produce the neurotransmitters dopamine and norepinephrine.

Pregnant women who are exposed to artificial chemicals called polychlorinated biphenyls (PCBs) may also have children with ADHD symptoms. PCBs were widely used in the United States until they were banned in the 1970s. Manufacturers used them in making fluorescent lights, pesticides, and finishes for wood floors, among other things. Traces of PCBs can still be found in places where they were once used or manufactured. Fish and other types of food, well water, and the air near these places may carry traces of PCBs. Exposure to PCBs during infancy can also put a child at risk for ADHD.

Very young children who are exposed to toxins (poisonous substances) in the environment may also be at increased risk for ADHD. One of these toxins is lead, which is found mostly in paint and pipes in old buildings. Lead poisoning has been shown to lead to disruptive or violent behavior and a short attention span. Some researchers believe that boys have a much greater chance of having ADHD than girls because testosterone, a hormone in their bodies, can make heavy-metal poisoning worse.

A 2008 study found that food colorings and a preservative (a chemical that keeps food from spoiling) called sodium benzo-ate caused children without ADHD to become hyperactive.

Some studies have indicated that food colorings, such as those found in gelatin desserts, could be linked to ADHD.

According to the APA, other things that can possibly cause or contribute to ADHD include a history of child abuse or neglect, multiple foster placements (when a child temporarily lives away from his or her parents with other adults who serve as foster parents), and infections such as encephalitis, which is caused by a virus that can make the brain swell.

Many people blame video games and other electronic devices for the high number of ADHD diagnoses. Video games and electronics don't cause ADHD, but researchers have found that children with ADHD who play a lot of video games can become addicted to them, and this addiction can lead to other addictive behaviors.

Some researchers point to sleep disorders as a factor in ADHD. Disorders in breathing during sleep, as well as restless leg syndrome (when a person can't stop his or her legs from moving in bed), are very often present when a person has ADHD.

Children with ADHD tend to become addicted to video games and other devices more easily than children without ADHD.

Symptoms such as restless leg syndrome and other sleep disorders may indicate to a family doctor that a child has ADHD.

IS IT REALLY ADHD?

Researchers and physicians caution parents that exposure to toxins (such as lead or secondhand cigarette smoke), sleep disorders, and thyroid problems can cause behaviors that resemble ADHD. The thyroid is a small gland at the base of the neck that converts iodine, which comes from many foods, into various chemicals. An overactive thyroid can cause hyperactivity and make a person distracted. An underactive thyroid can cause low energy and inattentiveness. Anemia, a condition in which the body does not have enough healthy red blood cells, often from a lack of iron, can also cause low energy, sluggishness, and inattentiveness.

Other conditions that can cause ADHD-like behaviors include depression, anxiety, and undetected seizures. A poor diet can also contribute to problem behaviors. Many children and adolescents don't have a balanced diet with the right mix of nutrients.

Calvin is in a regular elementary school classroom where he has been provided with some accommodations, or helpful aids. He sits on a large ball so he can rock on it instead of sitting completely still. Calvin's teacher also allows him to get up many times during the course of the day to sharpen his pencil or get a drink of water so he doesn't have to sit the entire time. He also attends a "friends class" in school to help him further develop his social skills and learn how to cope with stress.

Calvin is often overwhelmed by the sounds, sights, and textures around him. Rebecca and Dennis have used a variety of methods to make life easier for the family. At home Calvin has a special chair he can sit in away from other family members when he feels overwhelmed. Although sitting in the chair started out as a time-out, Calvin began to go to his chair by himself to calm down. Regular exercise is also critical for Calvin, because without it, he has trouble relaxing during the day and sleeping at night.

Rebecca and Dennis began taking Calvin everywhere they go with their family. Dennis says Calvin's progress is largely due to Rebecca's hard work in getting Calvin the correct diagnosis as early as possible and advocating for him. She has also worked with teachers and doctors to figure out which strategies help Calvin succeed. Rebecca and Dennis encourage other parents to do the same.

CHAPTER THREE

DIAGNOSING ADHD

Charles is a sixteen-year-old who was diagnosed with ADHD without hyperactivity when he was thirteen. "From a very early age, we could see that Charles was bright, mechanically inclined, and could figure out toys and projects without instructions," says Julia, Charles's mother. "He was also very creative and highly focused when working with electronics." As Charles got older, however, she and Chuck, Charles's father, began to notice that Charles was easily distracted and sensitive to sounds and touch. He also had difficulty following multistep directions when given them all at once.

Teachers told Charles's parents that their son was one of the smartest kids in class, but he talked too much and said things at inappropriate times. His grades were inconsistent, and he did not hand in assignments on time. Charles struggled with the increasing demands of school in seventh grade. He found it difficult to focus in class and couldn't manage to complete assignments on time. Charles says that before he was diagnosed, his grades went up and down a lot. "I would only pay attention to subjects I liked," he says.

Eventually, a child psychologist diagnosed Charles with ADD. Charles's pediatrician prescribed Concerta and Ritalin. Charles began taking the medications during the summer so he and his parents could see how they affected him.

THE PATH TO DIAGNOSIS

It can be very hard for doctors to diagnose children who are younger than five years old with ADHD. The behavior of children at this age is not as predictable as the behavior of older children. Many of the behaviors of young children without ADHD mimic the behaviors of older children with ADHD. A doctor might suspect ADHD if a young child is unable to sit still for activities that other children their age can enjoy, such as being read to by a parent. An early diagnosis is important if a child is going to be successful in school. Parents usually notice symptoms in their children, but often teachers are the first ones to recommend that a child see a professional. Teachers alert parents when a child's symptoms are negatively affecting his or her grades.

Parents speak up

How often parents spoke to school staff or health care providers about their children's emotional and behavioral problems in the past year.

■ Boys **▨ Girls**

Percentage of children whose parents talked about problems

18%

11%

Percentage took medication for ADHD symptoms

7%

3%

Source: National Center for Health Statistics

By Robert W. Ahrens, USA TODAY, 2008

Once parents and teachers decide that an evaluation is necessary, they contact someone who has experience with the disorder. Many different professionals can diagnose ADHD. These include:

- A psychologist (a professional who is not a medical doctor and who cannot prescribe medications but who understands the brain and can refer patients to medical doctors and psychiatrists)
- A psychiatrist (a medical doctor who can prescribe medications and other therapies for disorders of the brain)
- A pediatrician
- A family doctor
- A neurologist (a doctor who treats the brain and central nervous system)

- A counselor with a master's or doctorate degree in psychology or counseling
- A social worker
- A nurse practitioner (a specially trained nurse who can diagnose and assign treatment for diseases and disorders)

These professionals look at interactions with family members, schoolmates, teachers, and peers. They evaluate children and adolescents in different environments, such as at home and at school.

A doctor conducts an interview with a young patient. Diagnosing ADHD can be difficult and may require much time and the input of many medical and educational professionals.

The APA has a list of requirements to help professionals diagnose ADHD. These include:

- Ongoing inattention and/or hyperactivity/impulsivity that happens more often or is more severe than in other people of similar age
- Symptoms of any of the ADHD types before the age of seven causing some impairment (physical or mental weakness)
- Impairment from symptoms present in at least two different settings (for example, at home and at school)

- Evidence that the symptoms have interfered with performance in school, work, or age-appropriate social settings

THE DIAGNOSTIC INTERVIEW AND TESTING

An ADHD evaluation provides details about ADHD symptoms as well as any other conditions a person might have. One of the first things a doctor or other specialist should test for is disorders other than ADHD. They might test for disabilities (some of which can be identified by an IQ test), mood disorders, anxiety disorders, auditory processing disorders (which make it hard for a person to sort out sounds), and pervasive developmental disorders (PDD). A PDD involves delays in the development of many basic skills, especially the ability to socialize with others, communicate, and use imagination. A child with a PDD is often confused and generally has problems understanding the world around him.

Once other disorders are ruled out, parents and teachers fill out questionnaires called behavior rating scales. This process helps to identify any symptoms that might not have shown up during the interview and evaluation. Observation by an expert is another way to check for ADHD. Children with ADHD can be observed either at home, in school, or at a clinic. Clinics often have a playroom with a one-way mirror and a sound-monitoring system. A clinician observes the child working on tasks that are similar to tasks done at school or at home.

Often the clinician works for the school and observes the child in the classroom. When children are being observed at school, the teacher does not announce the professional's reason for being in the classroom, so the child being observed doesn't feel singled out. The professional also tries to observe all the activities in the classroom, not just the child under observation, so the child being observed doesn't feel self-conscious. Social services professionals who make home visits can also observe and report on what they find.

Researchers have developed a number of tests to help with diagnosis. While tests alone cannot diagnose a person with ADHD, they are useful when combined with information from the initial evaluation. One such test is the Continuance Performance Test (CPT). The person being tested sits at a computer. A series of letters or numbers appears on a screen, one at a time. The person being tested looks for a certain letter or number and has to hit a button or click the computer mouse when it appears. The CPT measures the individual's attention and impulsivity.

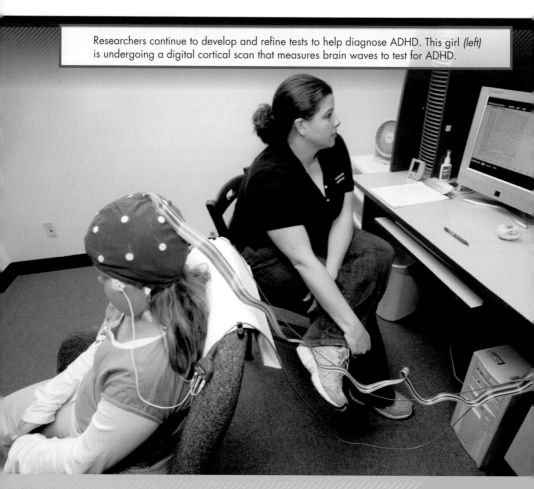

Researchers continue to develop and refine tests to help diagnose ADHD. This girl *(left)* is undergoing a digital cortical scan that measures brain waves to test for ADHD.

www.usatoday.com

USA TODAY

News

SECTION A

April 17, 2009

From the Pages of USA TODAY

Role of drugs, pharmaceutical industry examined

As a nutritionist and mother of a son with attention-deficit hyperactivity disorder, I believe that it is essential to view the use of drugs as one component of a multidimensional approach to this condition.

The importance of a wholesome diet rich in unprocessed whole grains, fresh fruits and vegetables, and containing minimal sugar, cannot be overstated. Subtle food allergies can mimic or exacerbate the symptoms of ADHD and should be ruled out or addressed. Omega-3 fatty acids are very supportive of the brain and nervous system and should also be included in the diet. These actions, along with carefully supervised use of medication, can often mean the difference between success and failure for those with ADHD. There is no one panacea [cure] for the problems these families face. Only a coordinated and health-oriented approach will suffice.

My son began using Adderall, an ADHD drug, eleven years ago in conjunction with the measures mentioned above. Today he is a 6-foot-2 [188 centimeters], successful college student preparing to graduate in June with a double major in biology and psychology. He intends to become a physician.

I urge all parents coping with this disorder to leave no stone unturned in managing it. And by all means they should feed their child well.

—Susan J. Machtinger, letter to the editor

Testing is sometimes required before a student can receive accommodations at school. Once the testing is completed, a doctor or other professional uses the information to make a diagnosis. He or she also suggests treatment, including therapy sessions or recommendations for medication. The final diagnosis should also include a list of necessary accommodations to be made by the patient's school or workplace. These accommodations can help the patient succeed.

SCHOOL AS A DIAGNOSTIC TOOL

Homework habits can be one of the most important indications that a child has ADHD. Many students with ADHD have difficulty beginning and completing their homework. They may also have a hard time keeping track of assignments or bringing home books and other materials they need to complete them. Once they do finish an assignment, they might lose it before they can hand it in.

A teacher's comments can be more important than grades when diagnosing ADHD. In addition to grades that seem lower than what the student is capable of, the following teacher comments may suggest that the student has ADHD:

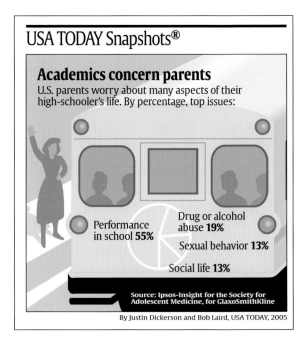

USA TODAY Snapshots®

Academics concern parents
U.S. parents worry about many aspects of their high-schooler's life. By percentage, top issues:

Performance in school **55%**

Drug or alcohol abuse **19%**

Sexual behavior **13%**

Social life **13%**

Source: Ipsos-Insight for the Society for Adolescent Medicine, for GlaxoSmithKline

By Justin Dickerson and Bob Laird, USA TODAY, 2005

- "Needs to try harder."
- "Doesn't work to potential."
- "Needs to pay attention better."
- "Doesn't hand in assignments."
- "Is disruptive in class."
- "Work is sloppy or rushed."
- "Doesn't follow directions."

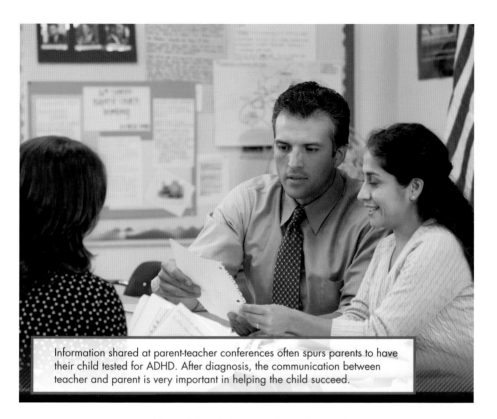

Information shared at parent-teacher conferences often spurs parents to have their child tested for ADHD. After diagnosis, the communication between teacher and parent is very important in helping the child succeed.

DIAGNOSING ADULTS WITH ADHD

At first experts considered ADHD to be a disorder only of childhood. But in the late 1970s, doctors started to diagnose the disorder in adults as well. There are a number of reasons for ADHD to remain undiagnosed until adulthood. ADHD was not well known twenty or thirty years ago when current adults were children. Some people are able to work around their ADHD symptoms when they are young, but have difficulty when they enter high school or college, or when they start a career. Very often adults with ADHD are unable to maintain strong relationships with other people. They may forget about important dates or tasks or they may be short tempered and easily frustrated. When doctors evaluate adults for ADHD they often want someone close to the patient, such as a girlfriend, spouse, or family

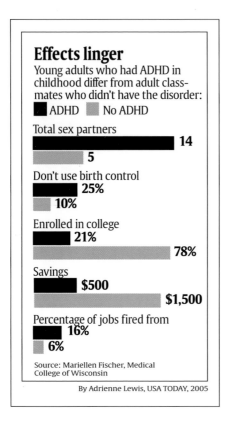

Effects linger

Young adults who had ADHD in childhood differ from adult classmates who didn't have the disorder:

■ ADHD   ▨ No ADHD

Total sex partners
14
5

Don't use birth control
25%
10%

Enrolled in college
21%
78%

Savings
$500
$1,500

Percentage of jobs fired from
16%
6%

Source: Mariellen Fischer, Medical College of Wisconsin

By Adrienne Lewis, USA TODAY, 2005

member, to take part in the process. The participation of this individual can help doctors to get a more complete picture of the patient. Particularly in the case of a spouse, the significant other can learn about ADHD and help his or her partner to cope, which will also improve their relationship.

In the first year following Charles's diagnosis, his doctor increased his Concerta dosage from 32 to 72 milligrams. Neither Charles nor his parents knew it, but this dose represented an overdose for Charles, who says it made him zombie-like. "I couldn't deal with it, so I just stopped taking the medication," he says. "But I didn't tell my mom. When I stopped taking it, I had tons of friends, but my grades suffered." It was an emotional day when Charles told his mother that he'd stopped taking his medication. "We argued," he says. "I told her that I couldn't have friends and good grades at the same time."

Charles went back to the doctor, who lowered his Concerta dose to 32 milligrams with a 5-milligram booster of Ritalin to help him do his homework. Charles hasn't had any side effects since the dosage was changed. He feels he's reached a good balance between his friends and his grades.

Getting diagnosed correctly with ADHD can be challenging for people with ADHD and their loved ones. The most important factor in getting an accurate diagnosis is a thorough evaluation by a professional who understands the disorder. Getting diagnosed correctly is the first step to a productive, fulfilling life.

CHAPTER FOUR

TREATMENT FOR ADHD

Jimmy is sixteen years old and in eleventh grade. Jimmy is in his third year of the Junior Reserve Officers' Training Corps program, which trains high school students to become officers in the U.S. armed forces. He is in honors classes at school and is working toward his black belt in karate. He was diagnosed with ADHD without hyperactivity when he was eight years old.

Jimmy takes Ritalin to help him focus. His medication dosing has changed as he's grown. For example, in second grade he was given a dose of time-released Ritalin in the morning. This means that the medication enters the bloodstream little by little over time. As he grew, his doctor added a non-time-released extra dose at noon. As he gained weight, his doctors increased and adjusted these doses if they were no longer effective.

Every summer, Jimmy stops taking the Ritalin because it makes it difficult for him to sleep. Jimmy would like to try to go to school without medication. The real test will be if he can focus on his honors classes without it.

TREATMENT OPTIONS

Treatment for ADHD can involve medicine, different kinds of therapy, and sometimes a combination of medicine and therapy. When an effective treatment is found, it should be carried out consistently on a long-term basis. Most people with ADHD do not grow out of it. Adults with ADHD may not have the same struggles as children with ADHD, but they still may need therapy. Specific therapies are required for people who have other conditions in addition to ADHD. For children with ADHD, parent education is a very important part of successful therapy.

Medication alone was once the only treatment available for people with ADHD. Medication can help to lessen symptoms. Doctors still prescribe medications to people with ADHD, but they are usually combined with some other type of therapy. Preschoolers benefit most from behavioral therapy without medication. But treatment programs that combine medications and therapy have been found to be the most effective in severe cases of ADHD in older children. Combination therapy is especially helpful to children who have trouble getting along with their peers. It has also been shown to be particularly effective in situations where ADHD symptoms cause a lot of stress in a family or when a child has another disorder, such as epilepsy or mental retardation, in addition to ADHD.

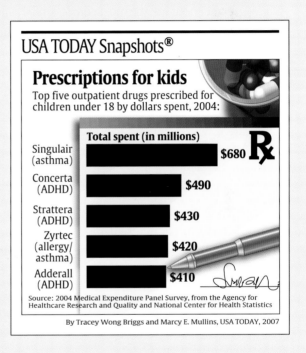

USA TODAY Snapshots®

Prescriptions for kids

Top five outpatient drugs prescribed for children under 18 by dollars spent, 2004:

Total spent (in millions)

Singulair (asthma)	$680
Concerta (ADHD)	$490
Strattera (ADHD)	$430
Zyrtec (allergy/ asthma)	$420
Adderall (ADHD)	$410

Source: 2004 Medical Expenditure Panel Survey, from the Agency for Healthcare Research and Quality and National Center for Health Statistics

By Tracey Wong Briggs and Marcy E. Mullins, USA TODAY, 2007

MEDICATION

ADHD medications help people focus, work, and learn. They can also improve physical coordination. A study by the NIMH found that students with ADHD who take medication tend to do better in math and reading than students who do not. The study also showed that children who were treated just with medication or with medication *and* behavioral therapy showed greater improvement than those who were treated with behavioral therapy alone. Medication is not meant to control behavior but to improve the symptoms of ADHD so that people with the disorder can function better.

Medications are the most controversial aspect of ADHD treatment. Many of them have dangerous side effects. But doctors can prevent or lessen side effects by changing the dosage—the amount of medicine taken at any one time. Doctors find out as much as they can about patients and their families so they are sure to prescribe the right medication. For example, a doctor would not prescribe Ritalin for a patient whose father had a history of heart disease. The side effects of Ritalin include making existing heart problems worse or even causing heart problems.

Each person's medication needs and responses are different. Some people might not need to take medication all the time. Others may need to try different medications if the first ones don't work or cause too many side effects. Other conditions (such as anxiety or depression) need to be taken into account when a person isn't performing very well on a certain medication. If a person has another condition in addition to ADHD, he or she may need to take more than one medication. Medications can be in the form of pills, powders, or patches worn on the skin.

ADHD is commonly treated with stimulants. Stimulant medications boost dopamine and norepinephrine levels in the brain. Stimulant medications prescribed for ADHD include methylphenidate (which has several brand names, including Ritalin and Focalin), Metadate, Concerta, Daytrana, Adderall, Vyvanse, and Dexedrine (also called d-amphetamine).

Stimulant medications can be short-acting or long-acting. Short-acting medications may stay in a person's system for four to six hours

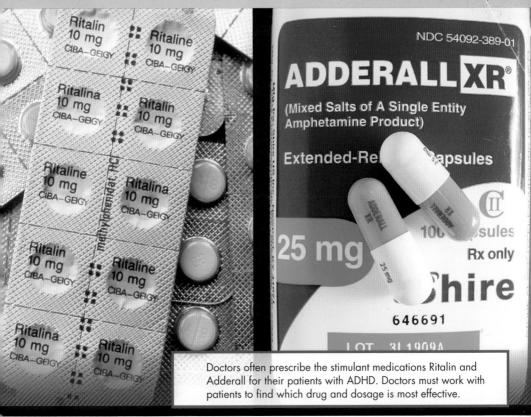

Doctors often prescribe the stimulant medications Ritalin and Adderall for their patients with ADHD. Doctors must work with patients to find which drug and dosage is most effective.

and need to be taken two or three times a day. The level of medication can go up and down in the body, which can lead to unevenness in a person's ability to focus. Most of the newer medications are long-acting and need to be taken only once a day. Children may need to have their doses adjusted over time as their weight increases and their medication loses its effectiveness at the original dose.

Some people who take long-acting medications may also need a small dose of a shorter-acting medication at the end of the day to avoid feeling irritable or experiencing a crashing feeling as their medication wears off. Each person's medication needs are different. Some need short-acting medications. Others need long-acting ones. Some people need a combination of both. Stimulant medications have been shown to improve concentration in 75 to 95 percent of people with ADHD.

www.usatoday.com

News
SECTION A

July 1, 2009

From the Pages of USA TODAY

Sudden death in kids, ADHD drugs linked

Stimulants used to treat attention deficit hyperactivity disorder could increase the risk of sudden death in children who have no underlying heart conditions, researchers report.

Such drugs have carried warnings since 2006 about an increased risk of sudden death in children or teens known to have serious heart abnormalities. But this is the first study to link the stimulants to sudden death in otherwise healthy young people, say officials of the Food and Drug Administration [FDA], which helped pay for the research. Further research is needed to confirm the finding, they said.

Columbia University scientists compared stimulant use in 564 young people who suffered sudden unexplained death with that of 564 killed in car accidents. They ranged in age from seven to nineteen and died between 1985 and 1996.

Researchers excluded subjects with

Non-stimulants are another group of drugs that can be used to treat ADHD. The non-stimulant medication Strattera can help people with ADHD, but it can take three to four weeks to begin working. Other non-stimulant drugs used to treat ADHD are clonidine and guanfacine. Clonidine decreases the symptoms of hyperactivity and impulsiveness and is often prescribed in combination with Ritalin, which treats symptoms of inattention.

Antidepressants are another class of medications used to treat ADHD. Antidepressants are commonly used to treat depression. Many antidepressants have not been studied for use in children and adolescents, so their effects are not well known. Doctors will prescribe antidepressants only for children with ADHD who don't identified heart abnormalities or a family history of sudden unexplained death. They interviewed parents and looked at autopsy reports to determine whether the victim had a heart abnormality or had been taking an ADHD stimulant drug.

Of those who died suddenly for no apparent reason, ten (or 1.8%) had been taking methylphenidate, sold under the brand name Ritalin. Only two (or 0.4%) who died in a car accident had been taking a stimulant, and only one of them had taken methylphenidate.

"It's hard to characterize the results as reassuring," the FDA's Robert Temple said at a news conference. Still, Temple said it's possible that the study missed stimulant use by the car-accident victims, because the parents of children whose deaths were unexplained might have better recall years later of what drugs they took.

"It's not a robust finding," he said, noting that if only one more automobile victim had been found to have taken an ADHD stimulant, the difference between that group and the sudden unexplained death group would no longer have been statistically significant. But, Temple said, "that doesn't mean that this is off the table and we're not concerned about it anymore."

The FDA is conducting two studies, one in children and one in adults, whose use of ADHD medications has been increasing, to see whether the drugs are associated with a higher risk of sudden death, heart attack, or stroke.

An estimated 2.5 million U.S. children take ADHD stimulants, according to an editorial accompanying the study, published online by the *American Journal of Psychiatry*.

—Rita Rubin

respond to stimulants or can't tolerate their side effects.

MEDICATION SIDE EFFECTS

Side effects of ADHD medications include decreased appetite, stomachaches, headaches, and difficulty sleeping. They can also cause tics and personality changes. Stimulant medications can be addictive and cause sleep disorders. To help patients who have trouble sleeping,

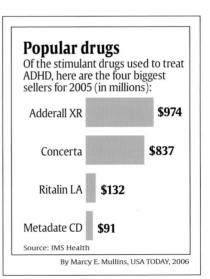

Popular drugs

Of the stimulant drugs used to treat ADHD, here are the four biggest sellers for 2005 (in millions):

Adderall XR	$974
Concerta	$837
Ritalin LA	$132
Metadate CD	$91

Source: IMS Health

By Marcy E. Mullins, USA TODAY, 2006

doctors may prescribe a lower dose of the medication. They may also instruct parents to give the medication to their child earlier in the day or to stop the afternoon or evening dose. Doctors often add a prescription for a low dose of an antidepressant or clonidine to help patients sleep at night.

The U.S. Food and Drug Administration (FDA) is responsible for ensuring the safety of the food supply and human and veterinary drugs. The FDA found that about one in one thousand people who take ADHD medications have a slightly increased risk for psychiatric symptoms such as feeling paranoid, behaving aggressively, and hearing voices. People with a psychiatric condition called bipolar disorder should not take stimulants, because stimulants can cause them to become manic (having intense feelings of happiness, extreme irritability, extreme impulsiveness, and other symptoms).

Children and teenagers who take the non-stimulant medication Strattera and some antidepressants are at increased risk for having suicidal thoughts. Parents, family members, and teachers need to watch these children's behavior carefully. Symptoms, which can crop up suddenly, can include acting more withdrawn than usual, acting very depressed, talking about hurting oneself, and having feelings of hopelessness or worthlessness.

Strattera and other non-stimulant medications can be helpful for people with mild ADHD and also depression or anxiety. They can also help people who can't take stimulants because they have heart problems. Clonidine and guanfacine can make people sleepy. Since clonidine is frequently prescribed to treat high blood pressure, children and adults with heart defects should not take it.

Companies that make ADHD medications issue medication guidelines that alert patients about possible risks. These risks include cardiovascular (involving the heart) and adverse (negative) psychiatric events. Pharmacists supply the guidelines to patients, families, and caregivers with their medications. People should always talk to their doctors if they have concerns about side effects.

Other drawbacks to treating ADHD with medications alone include what researchers call limited effects. This means that some children who take stimulant medications (up to 30 percent) show no clear benefit. The possibility of drug abuse is another cause for concern.

DRUG ABUSE AND ADHD MEDICATIONS

The impulsiveness of people with ADHD can lead to addiction. Often people with ADHD are drawn to addictive substances such as alcohol, street drugs, nicotine, and sugary foods. These addictions represent a negative way to cope with having ADHD.

Teens who take stimulant medications for ADHD are less likely to abuse other drugs than teens with ADHD who don't take the medications. However, some patients can become addicted to the medications they take to treat ADHD, but experts say that parents shouldn't worry about addiction if medications are monitored by a doctor and are taken as instructed. If doctors suspect their patients are addicted to a prescription drug such as Ritalin, they will try to find an alternative medication that has less (or no) potential for addiction.

However, some students who do not have ADHD seek out the medications used to treat it. One study found that 25 percent of kids with legal prescriptions for Ritalin had been approached by other kids asking to buy the pills. About 20 percent said they had sold or traded away at least one pill.

Some people find that medications work just fine in treating their ADHD. Others prefer different types of therapy, especially if they don't want to use medications or have experienced negative side effects from ADHD medications. One option is for people to take

www.usatoday.com

News
SECTION A

March 23, 2006

From the Pages of USA TODAY

ADHD pills may get new labels; will new attitudes follow?

Fidgety, unable to pay attention, disruptive and impulsive. Those terms might describe brief phases of virtually anyone's childhood. Or they could be symptoms of attention deficit hyperactivity disorder (ADHD).

With a staggering 3.3 million American kids taking powerful stimulant drugs to treat the disorder, a Food and Drug Administration advisory committee recommended Wednesday that warning labels more clearly alert parents to rare but serious risks of heart attacks, hallucinations and other psychological problems. The panel rejected calls for even stronger labels; people who need the drugs might be scared away.

The panel's action is the latest measure of concern that ADHD drugs such as Ritalin, Concerta, and Adderall are overprescribed.

When 63 percent of children in a single Virginia school district are diagnosed as having ADHD, it seems clear that, at least in some locations, they are. This invites side-effects, such as insomnia, tension, or drug dependency. It also means the true problem might go untreated.

But the frequency of misdiagnosis is a mystery. ADHD doesn't show up on X-rays or blood tests. It's a series of behaviors that

medications only when they are in school or are expected to perform in some other way that requires consistent focusing and attention.

Jimmy has a love-hate relationship with the medication. "I like to think of ADHD as digging a hole with your bare hands," he says. "The medication is like adding a shovel to dig. It's easier to get it done with less effort."

Of course, Ritalin doesn't solve everything. Jimmy also has a lot of support at home and in school. Jimmy is fortunate because a number of has to be examined in context and evaluated subjectively. Parents often learn that their child might have ADHD when a teacher informs them of suspected behavior.

This raises suspicions: Are some teachers using ADHD to control unruly students, particularly boys, who are naturally more rambunctious? Are parents seeking an edge for unfocused children who are struggling academically? Are time-pressed doctors handing out prescriptions based on little more than a fifteen-minute chat and a teacher's note?

Experts vehemently disagree about overprescription and whether the risks outweigh benefits. But if guidelines issued in 2001 by the American Academy of Pediatrics (AAP) were rigorously followed, much of the debate would fade. Those guidelines call on doctors to collect a child's medical, developmental, and educational history, plus behavior reports from the home and school.

That all takes time and money, of course, in a society that likes fast fixes and magic pills. It also can't be achieved with hard and fast rules. Rather, it requires a systematic attempt to change attitudes, so that the drugs are not the instant choice.

In this, the experience with antibiotics is instructive. Overuse has made some bacteria resistant, creating "superbugs" that could make some infections untreatable. Public health campaigns starting a decade ago raised awareness of this, and early studies suggest that doctors are getting more comfortable resisting patients' demands for antibiotics. A similar shift with the ADHD drugs might help curb their use and misuse.

There's also a risk in letting fears stop parents from giving their children medicine that could turn their lives around. About 70 percent of patients see improvement after taking the drugs, AAP notes. Children who go untreated for ADHD are more likely to use illicit drugs, drop out of school, and have other problems.

Calibrating the right balance on ADHD will depend less on the actions of regulators and more on the attitudes of parents, teachers, and doctors.

—*USA TODAY's editors*

people help him to cope with his disorder. Jimmy struggles with feeling that he has to take medication because he is somehow less capable than he should be. "We work hard to get him beyond that," says his mother, Kim.

Many staff members at Jimmy's school have been supportive and helpful. For example, Jimmy's school counselor has helped Jimmy look at himself not as having a handicap but as someone who is able to do things differently. Both his drill team coach and his karate instructor have taught Jimmy how to stay on task and focus.

www.usatoday.com

USA TODAY

News
SECTION A

January 17, 2008

From the Pages of USA TODAY

Baseball's ADD epidemic

Baseball, at the major league level, requires incredible concentration. Your attention can't be wandering if you're playing center field, or when a pitcher is throwing a 95-mile-an-hour [153 km/h] fastball in your direction.

So it was rather surprising to learn Tuesday of an apparent epidemic of attention deficit disorder among ballplayers who made it to the major leagues.

An epidemic, of course, would be the only legitimate explanation for the fact that last year 103 players—nearly four times as many as in 2006—sought "therapeutic exemptions" that would allow them to take controlled substances such as Ritalin and Adderall.

Because this disorder isn't contagious, a more plausible, and depressing, explanation for the spike is that many players were faking a medical condition so they could legally take stimulants and get around the ban on amphetamines that went into effect in 2006.

The startling statistics—disclosed by Representative John Tierney (Democrat, Massachusetts), at a congressional hearing focused on baseball's attempts to dig its way out of its long-running steroid scandal—suggest yet another drug problem in the tarnished national game.

Commissioner Bud Selig and players union chief Don Fehr, on whose watch the debacle occurred, insisted that they are taking responsibility for the steroid problem and moving to implement recommendations from former senator George Mitchell's unblinking report a month ago.

But it's tough to take them seriously when neither seemed particularly shocked by those attention-deficit numbers. If 103 players (7.6% of the league) are suffering from the disorder, it's striking baseball at a rate nearly 75 percent higher than in the general population.

Amphetamines (the players call them "greenies") have been a problem in baseball for decades. Now, nearly two years after they were banned, baseball can't shake the taint. Players and owners just don't get it. Fans want clean competition—untainted by steroids, amphetamines, prescription-drug abuse, and anything else that puts rule-abiding players at a disadvantage.

The news for baseball isn't likely to get better any time soon. Star pitcher Roger Clemens, who vehemently denied allegations in Mitchell's report that he used performance-enhancing drugs, was scheduled to testify under oath before the congressional panel.

—USA TODAY's editors

Kim, who has ADHD herself, firmly believes the disorder is hereditary, but she says, "I don't see it as a deficit [a handicap]." One tool that Kim uses to help her son is a software program called Family Access, which allows her and Jimmy to track how he's doing in school. The program allows Kim to see Jimmy's grades, how much money he's spending, his attendance, whether he has any missing homework assignments, and if he's been sent to the principal's office.

Jimmy's brother is completing basic training in the U.S. Air Force and will become an aircraft mechanic. He's reached his goals with mild ADHD and no medications. Jimmy hopes to follow in his brother's footsteps.

BEHAVIORAL THERAPY

Behavioral therapy focuses on specific behaviors in different social settings. The goal of this type of therapy is to help people with ADHD manage their symptoms. Therapists evaluate specific behaviors that cause problems in a person's life at school, at home, or in public and help the person build skills to manage those behaviors.

Before therapy begins, a mental health professional interviews the patient and collects information from parents and teachers. Together they develop a therapy program to target the specific needs of the patient. An effective program helps an individual be more attentive and treats specific problems that cause inattentiveness. The program should help to nurture the individual's strengths. Behavioral therapy programs focus on one or more of the following:

- Improving motor function (balancing, coordination, and movement), which helps patients control their bodies in healthy, age-appropriate ways
- Increasing ability to plan and organize actions and thoughts
- Learning appropriate responses to and understanding sensations from the environment

A child therapist meets with a girl and her mother to begin behavioral therapy. Behavioral therapy helps people with ADHD manage their symptoms.

- Building self-confidence
- Improving family interaction
- Creating a healthy environment (in both social interactions and the physical environment)

The effectiveness of behavioral therapy differs from person to person. When it does work, the therapy can help with other disorders a child might have in addition to ADHD. Behavioral therapy is especially useful for mild cases of ADHD, for preschool-age children with ADHD, and when the child's family prefers behavioral therapy to medication therapy.

Children also receive training in social skills, especially in the area of peer relationships. Counselors often hold group sessions that teach social skills to children. This type of training usually happens along with parent and teacher training, so that adults can reward or discipline children for good or bad behaviors. Adults with ADHD need help focusing at work and building relationships. Working with a therapist can help them to be successful in both areas.

Many people receive only medication as therapy for their ADHD because their insurance won't cover behavioral or other therapies or their communities don't have any professionals who practice behavioral therapy. Most doctors and researchers agree that the most effective therapy for ADHD is a combination of education, medication, and behavioral therapy.

BEHAVIORAL THERAPY FOR PARENTS

Behavioral therapy for parents is a proven strategy that helps young children with ADHD. Being the parent of a child with ADHD can be extremely difficult. Many parents do not know how to respond when their child with ADHD seems to ignore them or lashes out at them. Since many parents of kids with ADHD don't know any better, they react to these behaviors with harsh discipline or emotional or physical abuse. These negative parental behaviors have been shown to make ADHD behaviors worse.

Behavioral therapists teach parents and teachers special skills and techniques to improve a child's or teen's behavior. Children learn how to better interact with other people. Behavioral therapy also teaches the adults in a child's life how to interact with and discipline him or her effectively.

Behavioral therapy takes time and requires that adults be consistent. Parent training sessions cover a variety of issues, such as rules and structure at home, rewarding good behavior and withholding rewards or privileges for bad behavior, and planning ahead for going out in public. Since children with ADHD have difficulty adjusting to new routines or surroundings, parents must leave time for their children to adapt.

Parent training can take place in groups or within a family. Some families may need special approaches that are specific to the issues they face. Parents need to be involved with their child's school at all levels, including high school. Training can encourage better communication between parents and children, especially teenagers. Guidance counselors can help parents coordinate training for their child's teachers. School support staff and outside consultants can help teachers, and teachers can order training materials to help learn about strategies.

The organization Children and Adults with AD/HD (CHADD) provides a parent training program called Parent to Parent. The program provides educational information and support for individuals and families dealing with ADHD. The seven-week course provides information about ADHD, strategies for managing the impact of ADHD on the family, and tips on how to encourage positive behavior. Parents also learn about the educational rights of children with ADHD and how to speak up for their children.

Parents play an important role in every child's education. Their involvement is especially important for a child with ADHD.

BEHAVIORAL THERAPY FOR ADULTS WITH ADHD

Adults with ADHD can face difficulties in their work life and personal relationships. It is important for them to learn as much as they can about their disorder so they can develop strategies for success. Making lists and using computerized schedules can help. Some people place a large calendar with important dates and deadlines in a central location in the home or workplace. To avoid being distracted at work, adults with ADHD should keep their desks free of clutter. Open-design work spaces can be problematic for adults with ADHD. Employers can help by creating a work space with walls. Adjusting the hours one works can also help. Adults with ADHD might request starting work early. This way, they can get certain tasks done before their coworkers arrive, phones begin ringing, and e-mails start arriving. It is also helpful for adults to learn how to break down large tasks into smaller, manageable pieces.

Many adults with ADHD also need help with their social skills. They often have low self-esteem and a history of relationship problems. Adults might participate in individual counseling sessions as well as couples therapy. Mental health professionals can help adults with ADHD to improve communication skills and problem-solving abilities. Couples counseling can help the patient's partner to better understand ADHD so they can provide emotional support.

ALTERNATIVE THERAPIES

Complementary and alternative medicine (CAM) includes a wide range of therapies that are not included in traditional medicine. People use many different kinds of alternative therapies for ADHD. These include massage, herbal therapy, and treatment with nutritional supplements such as iron, zinc, and magnesium. Alternative therapies are not always supported by scientific research, but they can be effective.

Many parents and health professionals believe that the environment and nutrition can cause or worsen symptoms of ADHD. In particular, some people believe there are more kids with ADHD in the United States than in other countries because of changes in the environment. These changes include pollution in food, air, and water and a decrease in the nutritional content of food. The nutritional content of food has decreased as a result of modern farming practices. For example, a lack of organic fertilizer robs the soil of nutrients. Poor eating habits also affect nutrition, especially eating overprocessed foods with too much sugar and not eating enough vegetables and fruits. Experts believe that all these factors can cause problems with language, memory, attention, behavior, learning, and intelligence.

To counteract these environmental factors, CAM practitioners will do a series of blood tests to understand what might be triggering symptoms. For example, certain foods, such as dairy and wheat, might be removed from the patient's diet. Some patients avoid foods that might contain toxins, such as seafood that can contain mercury. If blood tests show low levels of nutrients such as iron and zinc, supplements are prescribed. Some doctors prescribe a combination of CAM therapy and traditional medication. This is known as integrative therapy. The CAM therapy treats symptoms while conventional medicine targets brain function. Unlike complementary or alternative medicine alone, there is often scientific evidence that integrative therapy is safe and effective.

NEUROFEEDBACK

Neurofeedback is a therapy that uses monitoring instruments to detect and change brain activity. Electrodes (sensing devices made up of small metal discs connected to wires) are connected to a computer at one end and attached to a patient's forehead at the other end. Researchers might have a child with ADHD play an educational video game while connected to the equipment. If the child playing the game continues to concentrate, the game continues, but if attention wanes, the game stops. This type of training helps children with ADHD who have problems with attentiveness and impulsiveness.

Some people question whether neurofeedback is a useful therapy for ADHD. Scientists are not exactly sure how it works, but it seems to have long-lasting benefits for people with ADHD and other disorders. Studies have shown that neurofeedback can have sustained benefits after treatment with Ritalin is stopped.

ADHD treatments vary, depending on the medical needs, preferences, and circumstances of each individual. Understanding as much as possible about the available therapy options can help individuals and their loved ones make informed decisions about which therapy will work best.

CHAPTER FIVE

COPING WITH ADHD

L exi is twenty-six years old. She was diagnosed with ADHD when she was twenty-five. In addition to ADHD, she was diagnosed with a borderline nonverbal learning disorder and borderline Asperger's syndrome. Lexi says she has always been impatient and impulsive. Throughout her school-age years, Lexi struggled with relationships, but she did very well with her academic studies.

When Lexi went away to college, things got better for her because diversity was something that was promoted on her campus. College made her more confident in herself, and she graduated with honors.

At the age of twenty-five, Lexi sought professional help because she was having trouble performing simple tasks. She worked as a bank teller. She was able to give out exact change, but became confused when asked to do multiple tasks. "My register wouldn't balance because I'd process the transactions wrong," she says. And although she never got fired at a job, these kinds of difficulties gave Lexi a low sense of self-worth.

After receiving her diagnosis, Lexi's doctor prescribed extended-release Ritalin. Lexi says the medication helped her a lot. She also says therapy increased her self-esteem. She worked with a licensed social worker. Over the course of six months, they formed a trusting relationship. "It was tremendously helpful to have someone to talk to, privately, about my worries about fitting in, how I didn't know what to do with myself after school, and how I even wondered if sometimes I was a good person because I was yelled at for behavior that I couldn't seem to stop," she says.

Earlier, Lexi had been diagnosed with anxiety and depression, "but it was the result of the ADHD and nonverbal learning disorder," she says. "I was depressed and anxious because I couldn't read people, I'd interrupt them, and I was really impulsive. A lot of that's cleared up."

Lexi takes Concerta for the ADHD, which she says works "fantastically," except that sometimes she needs additional medication in the evening to help her sleep. "Overall though, the benefit far outweighs the side effects," she says.

ADHD: AN EMOTIONAL ISSUE

ADHD can be frustrating for those who have the disorder and for the people who care about them. People with ADHD can feel very awkward around others, especially those who don't understand their disorder. Even peers, family members, and others who do know about ADHD can lose patience with those who have it. People with ADHD are often considered lazy, thoughtless, or insensitive. People with ADHD may feel rejected by others their age and may not have many close friends. Kids with ADHD may seem shy, withdrawn, aggressive, impulsive, or high-strung. Kids who have other disorders in addition to ADHD may face even greater difficulties with their peers.

Because ADHD is a disorder others can't see, it is often misunderstood. Sometimes people think that ADHD symptoms could be controlled if the person with the disorder would only try harder. This attitude can result in poor self-esteem for people with ADHD. They often do not expect to do well, which leads to failure. For example, if a student doesn't expect to do well on a math test, he or she might not study, which results in failure. If the student were encouraged to break the cycle by studying, he or she would likely improve. This change would affect self-esteem in a positive way.

Another important aspect of coping is known as self-care. This includes getting enough exercise, eating healthy foods, drinking enough water, and getting enough sleep. It may seem obvious that positive lifestyle habits can help someone cope with having ADHD,

Coping Strategies for Adolescents with ADHD

Limit distractions to stay focused. Sit toward the front of the classroom. Turn off e-mail, instant messaging, and the cell phone when doing homework or other tasks.

Work with your teachers. Talk to teachers about your ADHD. Work together to find learning strategies that work for you. For example, some schools will allow people with ADHD more time for taking tests. Ask if tutoring is available.

Get organized! Use tools that help you stay organized. For example, use a daily planner or smartphone *(right)* for help with remembering tasks and deadlines. Use

but it's not as easy as it seems. Being distracted and inattentive can cause a person to forget to get enough sleep or eat right, which can have a profound effect on his or her health and well-being. Another type of self-care is seeking out emotional support, such as peers, family members, and teachers. Some people with ADHD find it helpful to join support groups. Not getting enough emotional support (especially from peers) can lead to depression and anxiety, which can make ADHD symptoms worse.

a separate notebook to write down homework assignments and lists of materials you should bring home to do them.

Get moving! Physical exercise can help people who have ADHD. It helps to relieve excess energy.

Give yourself a break. If you tend to feel edgy during school, talk to a teacher about taking breaks from class so you can stay focused and concentrate better in class. Take frequent breaks while studying or doing homework.

Calm down. Practice relaxation, meditation techniques, and breathing exercises. They can help you relax and focus.

Talk to your friends. Let them know the situation. Help them to understand why you sometimes might say things without thinking them all the way through first. Apologize if you hurt anyone's feelings. Try to be careful with people you don't know well.

Sometimes routine tasks are frustrating for people with ADHD. Creating structure and routine in daily schedules helps to make things easier. For example, organizing a backpack, notebook, or locker at the same time each day can help people remember certain tasks. Getting rid of distractions in study areas and using a paper or electronic planner are good strategies for making organizational tasks easier. Parents and teachers can help children or teens with ADHD get organized and can lend support by reminding them to take their medications.

COPING IN SCHOOL

Students with ADHD often have trouble succeeding in school. In general, they have lower gradepoint averages. People with ADHD who go to college and are unable to manage their studies are sometimes placed on academic probation. This means they have a certain period of time to improve their grades or behavior or they will be expelled from school.

People with ADHD have trouble with time management, memory, organizing and finishing long-term projects, paying attention, and taking notes. Personal coaching is an effective solution for students with ADHD who need help with mental and physical organization. Professionals trained to treat ADHD can help students improve academic performance, learn to function in social situations, and increase self-esteem.

People with ADHD often use technology to help them stay organized or take notes. This smartpen and dot paper from Livescribe record what the user writes and hears for later use.

Education is an extremely important factor in helping people cope with and understand ADHD. Teachers need to be aware of strategies for helping kids with ADHD, many of whom are three or four years behind their peers in organizational, planning, and emotional skills. Teachers can help by using tools such as planners and other reminder systems to help students turn in homework on time.

Parents or professionals who coach kids with ADHD can help set academic and personal goals, create a plan of action, identify and develop personal strengths, and identify learning styles. Coaches can also teach students to report to another person on the goals and actions they've chosen to take, speak up and get the help they need, and identify what helps them to learn.

An especially challenging time for kids with ADHD is making the transition from grade school to middle school. Young children have just one teacher, but middle school students might have six or seven teachers per day. This means six or seven different teaching styles. In addition, the amount of homework increases and students are expected to get themselves to class on time.

Tools such as daily planners can help older students organize homework assignments. It also helps for kids to have two sets of textbooks, one at home and one at school, so they don't have to remember to carry the books back and forth.

Maintaining a positive attitude and self-image can be difficult for people with ADHD. Coaches work with students to identify what's going right in their lives and how to expand on those strengths. They identify positive role models, such as successful adults with ADHD.

Some schools are better able to accommodate students with ADHD than others. Lack of funding for teacher training and large class sizes can make it difficult for teachers to help students with ADHD. Students with ADHD who attend schools that don't educate their teachers about the disorder may find themselves caught in a never-ending cycle of being disciplined rather than getting the help and support they need.

Schools that do have resources often invest in training for teachers. In this case, everyone benefits because teachers have a better overall understanding of ADHD and can better cope with it in the classroom. One tool that has been proven to help students with ADHD in school is a daily report card (DRC). The DRC lists specific behavioral goals. Students who meet daily goals are rewarded at home. In the classroom, teachers can do many things to help students with ADHD. These include reducing task length, breaking large tasks into smaller units, making tasks more stimulating through the use of colors or textures, setting goals for students to achieve in short time periods, and tailoring instructions to students' learning styles. Teachers can also teach students with ADHD the skills they need to perform in school, such as note taking. Peer tutoring and computer-assisted instruction are other techniques that help students with ADHD. In peer tutoring, one student instructs another and provides assistance and feedback. This system increases academic as well as social skills.

When children reach adolescence, they can be much more involved in their own treatment process. They can work more directly with teachers, monitor themselves, be more independent at school, and work on their own organizational, time management, and homework issues. All this contributes to their self-esteem, which is one of the most important parts of coping.

Looking back, Lexi says, "I feel like the impulsivity of the ADHD really made me have so many snap judgments, especially with people that I shut out for fear of rejection as much as they actually rejected my actions for being weird." On the other hand, she says that being able to quickly make decisions has also helped her in some cases.

Lexi's husband has been a big help. "He's my best friend," she says. "He was very supportive when I was diagnosed," she says. "My parents don't believe I have a clinical problem."

In addition to being in a successful relationship, Lexi has gotten a job she loves at a well-known university. She has adopted a few strategies to stay organized at work. She has a written schedule, and she keeps to-do lists and whiteboards for her calendar and grocery list. She also uses an iPod touch to help her keep track of things. "I love my job at the university. Being able to work here and get my 'me time' when I'm studying or writing is a great help." Lexi is working toward an advanced degree.

HOW FAMILIES CAN COPE

The U.S. Centers for Disease Control and Prevention offer the following suggestions for parents and caregivers of people with ADHD:

- Recognize the importance of healthy peer relationships for children. These relationships can be just as important as grades to success in school.
- Maintain ongoing communication with people who play important roles in your child's life (such as teachers, school counselors, after-school activity leaders, and health-care providers). Be aware of your child's social development in community and school settings.
- Involve your child in activities with his or her peers. Communicate with other parents, sports coaches, and other involved adults about any progress or problems that may develop.
- Talk with program directors and your child's care providers about enrolling your child in a peer program, which can be especially helpful for older children and teenagers. Many

www.usatoday.com

USA TODAY

Life
SECTION D

October 20, 2008

From the Pages of USA TODAY

Children who have ADHD can strain marriages

Study: Extra stress is fuel for divorce

Parents of children with attention-deficit hyperactivity disorder are almost twice as likely as other parents to divorce by the time their child is 8 years old, a new study suggests.

A child's disruptive behavior doesn't in itself cause marriages to flame out, but it probably pours fuel on other stresses that spark marital conflict, say psychologists William Pelham Jr. and Brian Wymbs of the State University of New York-Buffalo.

In their study, 23% of parents had divorced by their child's eighth birthday if he had been diagnosed with ADHD, compared with 13% of similar parents in such factors as age, education and income whose child didn't have the disorder.

The study tracked divorces among 282 families with children who had attended a summer treatment program for ADHD symptoms. The children ranged from 11 to 28 years old at the time of the follow-up.

Pelham and Wymbs then examined how their parents' marriages had fared

schools and communities have such programs. A peer program is one that teaches high school students to offer peer mentoring, mediation (helping people solve disagreements and arguments), and tutoring to their peers. These programs teach participants communication and problem-solving skills, how to make decisions, and other life skills.

Parents must also be sure to pay enough attention to their other children who don't have ADHD, spending one-on-one time with compared with parents' divorce rates for a similar group of adolescents and young adults. The study is published in the October *Journal of Consulting and Clinical Psychology*.

"ADHD creates the greatest difficulty for parents in early childhood. If your marriage survives that, the rate of divorce doesn't continue to be higher after they're 8," Pelham says.

In Wymbs' lab studies, young actors imitate the behavior of children with ADHD and at other times act like ordinary kids as they do activities with married couples. The couples argue more and feel their partner is less supportive when they're with the child who acts as if he has ADHD.

Because ADHD can be inherited, parents often have it too, and that may hinder marriage, says Andrea Chronis-Tuscano, a psychologist at the University of Maryland. If children have ADHD, their mothers are 24 times more likely than other mothers to have it, and fathers are five times more likely, her studies find. Adults with ADHD may be impulsive and find it hard to concentrate or solve problems.

"That can lead to conflict in marriage," she says, "and a child with ADHD only adds to the stress."

In other studies, parents of children with ADHD have said they're less satisfied with marriage. But not all researchers agree that they divorce more. A large Canadian report last year found no higher divorce rate for parents of children with ADHD. Pelham's group may have particularly bad symptoms because their parents sought treatment, says Lisa Strohschein, a sociologist at University of Alberta who did the Canadian study.

Nonetheless, Pelham says doctors who diagnose children with ADHD should advise parents who need it to get couples counseling.

—Marilyn Elias

each of them to make sure they don't feel neglected. Parents should also encourage their children without ADHD to talk openly about their feelings. Parents should be aware of warning signs of possible anxiety disorders in their other children.

Family counseling can also help families understand how to interpret ADHD behaviors, how to interact with one another, what to expect or not expect, and how to cope emotionally with having a family member with ADHD. Support groups for children, teens, and young adults with ADHD and their families can also provide some much-needed emotional support for families that are coping with ADHD.

PARENT EDUCATION AND TRAINING

According to CHADD, parent education is essential to the treatment of ADHD. Parents should consider being trained to support their children with ADHD. CHADD encourages parents to be consistent and reward children for positive behavior. It also emphasizes the importance of teaching children problem-solving and communication skills.

Parent training programs can also raise awareness of triggers to negative behavior. Parents learn how to target and monitor problem behaviors and to reward good social behavior with praise, positive attention, and rewards. Strategies to decrease unwanted behavior include planned ignoring, time-outs for younger children, and removal of privileges for adolescents and teens. Participation in such programs often leads to an improvement in parent–child relationships.

SUPPORT GROUPS

Support groups can help people with ADHD feel less alone. Support groups offer a place where people with ADHD can go to meet other people who are dealing with the disorder. Participants can learn coping strategies and gain emotional support from people who have firsthand knowledge of the challenges they face. Parents and other family members can attend their own support groups. In these groups, people can learn and draw strength from others who have loved ones with ADHD.

Several national organizations with local chapters have support groups, such as CHADD and the Attention Deficit Disorder Association. Hospitals, schools, and universities often offer ADHD support groups. And in areas where support groups do not exist, some individuals start their own groups or join one online.

Parent Strategies to Help Children with ADHD

Create a routine. Try to follow the same schedule every day.

A place for everything and everything in its place. Always keep backpacks, clothing, and toys in the same place.

Minimize distractions. Turn off the TV and radio, especially when your child is doing homework. Whenever possible, have homework done away from the computer.

Limit choices. To avoid confusion or feelings of being overwhelmed, offer a choice between two things (this T-shirt, snack, activity or that one).

Keep it simple. Instead of long, detailed explanations, use clear, brief directions to remind your child of responsibilities.

Use goals and rewards. Set realistic goals. Use a chart to keep track of positive behaviors. Give rewards for effort, good behavior, and completion of tasks.

Time out! Avoid yelling or spanking. Use time-outs or withdraw privileges instead.

Nurture your child's talents. Finding out what your child does well (sports, art, music) and supporting it can boost social skills and self-esteem.

Famous People with ADHD

ADHD can be a difficult condition to deal with, but as many of the stories in this book demonstrate, learning how to cope with having ADHD can lead to a successful, fulfilling life. Experts believe that Thomas Edison, Albert Einstein, Henry Ford, Wolfgang Amadeus Mozart, Edgar Allan Poe, and Walt Disney all probably had ADHD. People who have openly discussed their disorder include Jim Carrey, Robin Williams, Michael Jackson, Joan Rivers, Axl Rose, Tom Cruise, Whoopi Goldberg, Steven Spielberg, and Patty Duke.

Thomas Edison *(left)* and Albert Einstein *(right)* are both believed to have had ADHD.

Many private and public schools offer summer camps designed for children with ADHD. The camps teach kids behavioral and social skills in a fun, casual environment. Some universities offer summer camps that provide social skills training and group problem solving to children and teens with ADHD. Some of the programs use daily report cards to track the progress of their students and a point

Students at a summer camp for people with ADHD stop to eat during a hike. The program is highly structured to best benefit its campers.

system with rewards and consequences. Many of the camps focus on peer relationships and appropriate behavior for school and work.

ADHD affects more than just people with ADHD. Coping with ADHD can seem like a difficult task, but there are many tools to help people with ADHD and their families cope more effectively. Not everyone chooses the same methods for coping with ADHD. The most important element in effective coping is education: all parties should learn as much as possible about ADHD so they can work together to help and support one another.

CHAPTER SIX

LAWS AND ADHD

Thomas is a tenth grader who was diagnosed with ADHD when he was in second grade. Before his diagnosis, Thomas had problems reading. He also had trouble spelling and copying words from the blackboard onto his paper. His teacher suggested testing Thomas's reading and learning abilities so she could better understand his strengths and weaknesses. After the testing, Thomas took special reading classes and did well in second through fourth grade.

But in fifth grade, Thomas started to do whatever he could to get out of the classroom. The noise level and number of kids in his class, the amount of new assignments, and the requirement that he manage his own work made him anxious. He would constantly display other task-avoidance behaviors such as putting his head down on his desk and pulling his hood over his head. To get away from the classroom (to relieve his anxiety), he would complain of headaches and light sensitivity, which landed him in the nurse's office quite often.

Thomas's parents took him to a lot of specialists, including a neurologist, an ophthalmologist (an eye doctor), and an audiologist (a doctor who treats hearing disorders), to rule out other things that might be wrong. As it turned out, Thomas discovered he did have a slight hearing disorder, but his primary diagnosis remained ADHD.

When Thomas started to show an increase in difficult behaviors in the fifth grade, his pediatrician increased his Concerta dose to 54 milligrams. This led to difficulty with sleeping and eating. Thomas developed dark circles under his eyes, his growth and appetite slowed down, and he was irritable and angry all the time.

Thomas's doctor changed his medications, and his parents took him to see a psychiatrist. The doctor took Thomas off Concerta and put him on Adderall XR and Trazodone, an antidepressant to help him *sleep. According to his mother, Kara, this was too much change all at once. The Trazodone "made him feel like he was crawling out of his skin." She partially blames the drug for an episode of major depression that caused Thomas to be admitted to the hospital. "Thomas began to talk about hurting himself if we asked anything of him," says Kara. "At first we thought he was just saying this to get out of a task, like going to school or karate. However, he really was talking about wanting to commit suicide."*

The doctors and counselors at the hospital worked with Thomas to sort out his feelings and to observe him. He was eventually diagnosed with anxiety disorder. He remained under the care of a psychiatrist and social workers and also met similar kids in group sessions. This program was followed by two and a half years of therapy, not just for Thomas but for his family.

U.S. federal laws protect the rights of many people with disabilities, including people with ADHD. The educational rights of children with ADHD are protected by two laws, the Individuals with Disabilities Education Act (IDEA) and Section 504 of the Rehabilitation Act of 1973. These laws help provide an appropriate education for students with special needs. Even colleges and universities are required

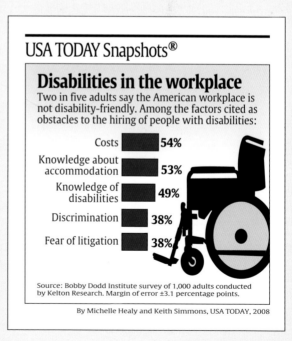

USA TODAY Snapshots®

Disabilities in the workplace

Two in five adults say the American workplace is not disability-friendly. Among the factors cited as obstacles to the hiring of people with disabilities:

Costs	54%
Knowledge about accommodation	53%
Knowledge of disabilities	49%
Discrimination	38%
Fear of litigation	38%

Source: Bobby Dodd Institute survey of 1,000 adults conducted by Kelton Research. Margin of error ±3.1 percentage points.

By Michelle Healy and Keith Simmons, USA TODAY, 2008

USA TODAY

to help students with ADHD and other disabilities to overcome challenges and find success at school. The Rehabilitation Act of 1973 also helps adults with ADHD. This act and the Americans with Disabilities Act of 1990 (ADA) prohibit discrimination in the workplace against individuals with disabilities. The ADA also applies to school-age children in some cases.

THE INDIVIDUALS WITH DISABILITIES EDUCATION ACT

IDEA became law in 1990. The law ensures that U.S. children with disabilities receive services to help them be successful in school. The law has been updated several times since then. Part C addresses special services for children with disabilities from birth to the age of two. Part B of the law applies to people aged three to twenty-one.

When IDEA became a law in 1990, it did not apply to children with ADHD. But in 1991, the U.S. Department of Education directed schools to include ADHD as a covered disability under IDEA. An ADHD diagnosis does not guarantee that a student can qualify for services under IDEA. A student with ADHD must have a condition that meets one of thirteen disabilities outlined in the law. The requirements set forth in IDEA are very strict. For the individual to receive services, a student's disability must affect academic performance.

IDEA ensures that everyone receives a "free appropriate public education," regardless of ability, by protecting the rights of students with disabilities. It entitles children to a comprehensive free evaluation by a team of specialists at no cost to parents.

Special education services meet the needs of each child individually. These services include individual or small group instruction, technology that assists children with special needs (such as laptop computers that allow children who can't speak to communicate by writing what they want to say), speech and physical therapy, and changes to lesson plans used in classrooms where children with special needs are present. Each child who receives special education services has an Individualized Education Program (IEP).

THE INDIVIDUALIZED EDUCATION PROGRAM

An IEP is a document that includes goals tailored for a specific child. According to the National Resource Center on ADHD, the IEP should state the following:

- Grade level
- Which services will be granted
- When services will be provided
- How long services will last
- How frequently services will be provided
- How a child's progress will be measured

Sometimes a child's behavior prevents learning or disrupts the learning of other students in the class. In this case, the IEP team must consider the use of positive behavioral interventions and supports or other strategies to address the behavior.

The IEP is developed by a team that includes the student's teachers, parents, the student (if appropriate), and a representative from a local education agency who can supervise the special education services. The team can also include anyone else the parents or student requests. IEPs are reviewed annually.

IDEA requires that parents receive written notice before any major changes are made to a child's placement or services. Also, educational institutions must provide impartial hearings for parents who disagree with identification, evaluation, or placement decisions made for their child.

SAMPLE IEP
FOR SCHOOL-AGE CHILD WITH ADHD

This excerpt from an IEP for a middle school girl shows the kind of information the IEP committee members gather when they evaluate the needs of a student with ADHD.

Confidential Student Information

SCHOOL-AGE Individualized Education Program (IEP)
School: Glendale Middle School

Student Name: Jessie McCabe | **Date of Birth:** 03/16/97 **Age:** 13 **Grade:** 7

Disability Classification: Learning disabled / ADHD

Date of initial referral: 09/20/2010
Date of IEP meeting to determine initial eligibility: 10/01/2010

Date of Committee on Special Education (CSE) Meeting to Develop this IEP: 10/20/2010

Type of Meeting:
X Initial ☐ **Requested Review** ☐ **Annual Review** ☐ **Reevaluation**
Date IEP is to be Implemented: 11/01/2010; **Projected Date of Next Review:** 04/01/2011

Attendees:
School psychologist: Josephine Roberts
Principal: Mark Powell
Teacher: Lynn Smith
Teacher: Melissa Jones
Parent: Fred McCabe
Parent: Wilma McCabe

Student Strengths:
Positive responses to reinforcement programs
High level in mathematics
Desire to do well
Enjoys art and music

Current Student Needs

Parent Concerns:
Below grade level in reading
Difficulties with spelling and writing
Takes a long time to complete homework
  assignments
Forgets assignments or materials/books at school

Teacher Concerns:
Behavior issues in the classroom, can be disruptive
Problems with fluency in reading
Poor spelling and writing skills
Does not turn in assignments on time
Does not fully complete assignments

Present Levels of Academic Achievement, Functional Performance and Individual Needs

ACADEMIC ACHIEVEMENT, FUNCTIONAL PERFORMANCE AND LEARNING CHARACTERISTICS:
Current levels of knowledge and development in subject and skill areas, including activities of daily living, level of intellectual functioning, adaptive behavior, expected rate of progress in acquiring skills and information and learning style.

In reading, student is currently testing on a 5.5 grade level.
Difficulty with comprehension. For example, Jessie can read through a paragraph, but does not retain the information.
Also has trouble grasping concepts without individual help.
Student is currently working on grade level in math.

Confidential Student Information

SOCIAL DEVELOPMENT:
The degree and quality of the student's relationships with peers and adults, feelings about self and social adjustment to school and community environments.

> Jessie gets along well with classmates, but can be disruptive. She exhibits hyperactive behaviors and has difficulty focusing.
> Teacher has experimented with giving spelling tests orally rather than written. This seems to help.

PHYSICAL DEVELOPMENT:
The degree or quality of the student's motor and sensory development, health, vitality and physical skills or limitations that pertain to the learning process.

> Not applicable

Measurable Annual Goals

Annual Goal: What the student will be expected to be able to do by the end of the year in which the IEP is in effect.
Evaluative Criteria: How well and over what period of time the student must demonstrate performance in order to consider the annual goal to have been met.
Procedures to Evaluate Goal: The method that will be used to measure progress and determine if the student has met the annual goal.
Evaluation Schedule: The dates or intervals of time by which evaluation procedures will be used to measure the student's progress.

ANNUAL GOAL: Will be reading on a 6th grade level by 04/30/2011	
Procedures to Evaluate Goal:	Use current testing procedures
Evaluation Schedule:	Test between 4/15/2011 and 4/25/2011 so results will be available for follow-up meeting on 4/20/2011.

(Add additional annual goals as appropriate)

Recommended Programs And Services

Program/Service	Frequency	Duration	Location	Initiation Date
Extra set of books at home	N/A	Until the end of the school year	N/A	Immediately
Seating in front of classroom	Every day	Until review of IEP	Regular classroom	10/21/2010

TESTING ACCOMMODATIONS:
The following individual appropriate accommodations are necessary to measure the academic achievement and functional performance of the student on State and districtwide assessments. Recommended testing accommodations will be used consistently in the student's education program, in the administration of districtwide assessments of student achievement, consistent with school district policy, and in the administration of State assessments of student achievement, consistent with State Education Department policy.

TESTING ACCOMMODATION	CONDITIONS	SPECIFICATIONS
Provide spelling tests orally	Weekly, for the remainder of the school year, in the resource room	Begin 10/21/2010
Extend time for completing tests	Weekly, for the remainder of the school year, in the regular classroom	Begin 10/21/2010

SECTION 504 OF THE REHABILITATION ACT OF 1973

Children who are not eligible for services under IDEA may qualify under Section 504 of the Rehabilitation Act of 1973. The Rehabilitation Act originally prohibited discrimination against adults who were government employees or who worked for organizations that were funded by federal monies. Section 504 is a civil rights law that protects people with disabilities from discrimination in any program or activity that receives money from the U.S. government, such as a school. Most schools, including public colleges and universities, receive federal funding and are covered under Section 504.

Like IDEA, Section 504 guarantees a free and appropriate education to all children, no matter what their disabilities. Unlike IDEA, however, it does not have specific criteria for eligibility or provide guidelines for creating an IEP. So while Section 504 covers more children, it doesn't provide as many services. Its main focus is making sure that students with disabilities receive the same services as students without disabilities, whereas IDEA defines a free and appropriate education as specific to each student's individual needs.

A 504 Plan is a legal document that outlines a plan for students in the general education setting. Before receiving a 504 Plan, a child must have an evaluation that includes information from a variety of sources, such as parents, teachers, test scores, doctor notes, and so on.

Students with ADHD often have a 504 Plan. The National Resource Center on ADHD provides the following examples of appropriate accommodations for children with ADHD:

- Reducing the number of homework problems without reducing the level or content of what is being taught
- Giving the student a quiet place to work or a place without many distractions
- Providing clear and simple directions for homework and in-class assignments

- Giving tests in a quiet place and/or providing extra time
- Letting the student use a tape recorder or giving the student a copy of notes
- Using behavior management techniques, including positive reinforcement
- Having a nurse or administrator oversee a student's medication
- Having the student meet with the school counselor
- Keeping parents informed of the child's progress or difficulties

AMERICANS WITH DISABILITIES ACT

The purpose of the ADA is to protect people with disabilities from discrimination. The ADA built on the Rehabilitation Act, extending beyond government employees. It applies to private employers with fifteen or more employees, all activities of state and local

President George H. W. Bush signs the Americans with Disabilities Act in 1990. The act protects people with disabilities from discrimination. People with documented ADHD can use the law to fight discrimination at work or at school.

governments, including employment, and so-called places of public accommodation, such as private schools and colleges.

To be considered disabled under the ADA, a person must have a physical or mental condition that limits life activities, and the problem must be documented (for example, in doctors' records). To be covered by the ADA, a person must show that discrimination occurred because of a disability of more than six months. The ADA applies to all educational institutions, even those that do not receive federal funding.

With regard to students, the ADA does not require an organization to provide a free appropriate public education. The act does, however, limit separation of students with disabilities from those without disabilities. For example, a student with a disability has the right to choose between playing in an athletic league for students with disabilities or a regular league, if he or she is qualified to play and that choice is available. "Reasonable accommodations" include redesigning equipment, assigning aides, providing alternative formats for written material, modifying tests, altering existing facilities, and building new facilities.

The law was created so that people with disabilities can have equal access to jobs, housing, public

USA TODAY Snapshots®

Hiring the disabled

What companies believe are the greatest barriers to hiring the disabled:

Type of work cannot be performed by the disabled	32%
Employer discomfort or unfamiliarity with hiring people with disabilities	10%
Cost of accommodating the disabled	5%
Fear of litigation under the Americans with Disabilities Act	4%
Lack of knowledge or information on the disabled	37%

Source: Heldrich Work Trends Survey of 501 personnel directors, human resource directors and executives responsible for hiring. Margin of error ±4.38 percentage points.

By Darryl Haralson and Sam Ward, USA TODAY, 2003

Section 504 of the ADA requires schools to make reasonable accommodations for students with ADHD. These may include one-on-one aides in the classroom.

places and services, and other areas that have an important impact on their lives.

One summer when Thomas was about thirteen, Kara investigated a local summer camp for kids with ADHD. She went to meet the director, who introduced her to the organization known as CHADD (Children and Adults with ADHD). Kara and Harry, Thomas's father, then discovered the missing piece of Thomas's treatment: parental support. They realized the importance of becoming educated about ADHD and how it was affecting Thomas, and they realized they needed to learn how to advocate for Thomas and how he could advocate for himself.

Because of CHADD workshops, Thomas's teachers are also very knowledgeable about ADHD. They have worked closely with Thomas's parents to make many helpful accommodations for him. Thomas is now in smaller classes (under fifteen students). Thomas's teachers *allow him to do his homework in school so they can provide help if he needs it. With his homework done, Thomas faces less stress at home. Thomas's teachers also read test questions to him (because of his reading disability), do not take points off for spelling (because of his poor working memory), and, thanks to the IDEA, follow his Individualized Education Program in a regular classroom setting.*

Thomas's journey hasn't been easy. However, with many learned coping skills and assistance, he is doing much, much better. Thomas is learning karate, and he gets mostly As and Bs in school. A class in middle school that accommodated children with behavioral challenges helped Thomas develop confident leadership skills. He showed the way for the other students and was always the first to help them when they had a difficult day. With the love and support Thomas received from those around him, he became a model for his peers. "These qualities he's gained from his struggles should last a lifetime," says Kara.

WHO BENEFITS FROM THE LAWS?

All sections of these laws (IDEA, Section 504, and the ADA) do not apply to every person with disabilities. It depends on the person's age and disorders. To take full advantage of the laws and the help they provide, people must become advocates. Advocates support or promote their own interests or those of someone else. Parents often advocate for their children to get them appropriate services in school. Sometimes people with ADHD feel they are discriminated against at school or work. They can use the laws to get the support and help they need.

Some organizations try to get around these laws (especially the ADA, which applies to adults in the workplace), so they don't have to accommodate people with disabilities. The laws guarantee that people with disabilities have access to the same education, services, and facilities (buildings and other physical structures) that other people have. They ensure that people with disabilities are not separated from the rest of society.

IDEA and Section 504 apply to the education of children with disabilities. Students who need a wide range of services or protections would probably be best served by IDEA, which gives parents more rights and responsibilities in their child's education. Section 504 applies mainly to students who only need simple accommodations.

The ADA is mainly for adults. Young adults who have ADHD or other disabilities who are applying to colleges or universities should know about the ADA and what it does. It also applies to adults trying to find a job or a place to live on their own.

ADVOCACY AND ADHD

I have a son who is now seventeen with ADHD, and my biggest issue is the lack of help and guidance from the schools he attended from grade school on up to high school. In fact I do not know any school in the entire state that provides supports for these kids suffering from this disability. The only help they provide is a 504 Plan, but that is only minimal. Teachers and faculty do not have the training or patience necessary to see that these kids are offered the same education as the kids who don't have this issue. I have only hit roadblocks over and over from all these schools. It would be nice if they took extra time training teachers and educators about ADHD. My son has had so many bad experiences and has been suspended so many times, he now detests school and that has affected his choices for the future.

—Colorado mother of a seventeen-year-old with ADHD

It isn't always easy for parents to find the services that will help their children with ADHD to grow and prosper. As this mother's story clearly shows, not all school districts have the resources to help kids with ADHD in constructive ways. Some school districts have the resources, but staff members don't listen to parents. They pressure parents to put their children with ADHD on medications, which may not be the right decision.

ADHD is often the subject of a teacher-versus-parent debate. In this debate, teachers and parents argue about which of them is responsible for the special needs of kids with ADHD in the classroom. Most experts agree that it should be a combination of the two, and usually parents and teaching staff work as a team. But this isn't how it always works out.

Since parents never know exactly how schools will be able to help their children, they need to educate themselves about ADHD, what their children's rights are, and how to go about making sure their children get the services they need. Parents must understand how a diagnosis affects their child's performance at school and the education they receive and what can be done at home to help the child succeed.

Advocacy also means taking an active role in planning and understanding a child's IEP, not being afraid to interact with teachers and other staff, and asking questions. Parents also need to keep track of a sometimes overwhelming amount of paperwork, including reports, evaluations, and letters they send to school. In addition, they need to help their children come up with a system to keep track of homework and projects. In some cases, a parent might have to move a child to a different school if he or she isn't doing well or receiving services.

A parent may also have to educate the child's doctor. Not all doctors are knowledgeable about ADHD, and not every child fits into a one-size-fits-all mold when it comes to ADHD. Parents may also have to be advocates with neighbors, coaches, and others who might want to help a child but do not understand why the child acts the way he or she does.

Many groups advocate for the rights of people with ADHD. If parents can't find any resources nearby, national organizations such as CHADD can steer them in the right direction for information and support.

www.usatoday.com

USA TODAY

News
SECTION A

August 1, 2008

From the Pages of USA TODAY

Built to swim, Phelps found a focus and refuge in water

Kid who "never sat still" aims for eight more golds, Olympic history

Michael Phelps' remarkably long torso is like the hull of a boat, his coach says, allowing him to ride high on the water. His ankles, knees, elbows, and shoulder joints are rubber-band flexible. His wingspan is three inches [8 centimeters] longer than his six-foot-four [193 cm] height.

But for all of the genetic gifts that make him a master at defying drag in the water, for all of the physical advantages that could propel the twenty-year-old swimmer to the best Olympic performance of all time, the key to Phelps' superiority is what is in his mind as he races.

Very little.

"It's either nothing or 'I have to get my hand on the wall before they do,'" says Phelps, who won six gold and two bronze medals in the 2004 Olympics.

His coach says that single-mindedness, that ability to shut out the great expectations and the supercharged Olympic atmosphere, will allow Phelps—who will race up to 20 times in Beijing in pursuit of a record eight gold medals—to climb out of the pool each time with an eye only on what's next.

"That," coach Bob Bowman says, "is his strongest attribute."

For an athlete who took Ritalin for attention deficit hyperactivity disorder (ADHD) as a child, it is also his most surprising asset.

"Michael's ability to focus amazes me," says his mom, Debbie Phelps, a middle school principal who occasionally speaks on panels about ADHD.

Bowman, who began coaching Phelps at the North Baltimore Aquatic Club when the swimmer was 11, recalls how much time Phelps spent sitting near the lifeguard stand as a kid, benched because he was being too disruptive.

"He never sat still. He never shut up; he would never stop asking questions," his mom says. "He just wanted to go from one thing to another."

When he was in elementary school, a teacher told his mom that Phelps would never focus on anything. His mom disagreed. She had seen him at swim meets.

"He might be rocking on the kickboard as he's waiting to swim," she told the teacher, "but he knows what he wants to do."

Even then, Phelps pined to excel in the sport his mom initially chose for his energetic older sisters, Whitney and Hilary, who are twenty-eight and thirty.

"I don't want to lose," Phelps says. "That's the thing. If I don't want to lose, I can focus."

In Melbourne [2004 Summer Olympics in Australia], no one came close to running down Phelps. Even his mom couldn't believe it.

"I was in awe," she says. "It was like, 'Michael, what are you doing?'"

Through it all, Phelps says, his mind was focused on simply touching the wall first. Even in practice, he doesn't let his mind wander far. As he swims lap after lap, he says, he might sing a song in his head.

Michael Phelps holds one of his eight gold medals from the 2008 Summer Olympics in Beijing, China. Until he started swimming, Phelps, who had ADHD as a child, couldn't focus. Since then his focus has become his greatest asset as a world-class swimmer.

But his thoughts don't drift, he says, to his interests outside the pool, which include poker, video games, and his beloved English bulldog, Herman.

When he walks on the pool deck for a race, rap or hip-hop likely is pumping through his headphones. "(But) my mind is focused on the job that I have to do," he says.

"It's just easy for me to do that. I don't know why."

All his mom knows is that swimming set her hyperactive son on a singular path. He asked to be taken off Ritalin when he reached middle school, mainly because he didn't want to go to the school nurse's office each day. His mom agreed on the condition he wouldn't act up at school.

By then, Bowman had laid out a plan for Phelps, one that had a horizon as far as the 2012 Olympics, one focused lap at a time. Phelps never went back on Ritalin.

"Would you look back and say, would any sport have done that? Maybe so," Debbie Phelps says. "But swimming was Michael's comfort zone."

—*Vicki Michaelis*

CHAPTER SEVEN

ADHD RESEARCH AND THE FUTURE

Beth is a brilliant and funny sixty-eight-year-old psychologist who wasn't diagnosed with ADHD until she was in her sixties. Beth, a clinical psychologist, remembers daydreaming in elementary school and not paying much attention to what she was being taught. Since Beth was quiet and didn't cause trouble, her teachers would put her in the back of the classroom, where she would read novels and books about music.

Beth grew up on a farm but attended school in the city. She didn't have many friends in school, which made her feel different and isolated. School was a struggle, and she spent a lot of time wondering how she was ever going to survive it. Then in ninth grade, Beth remembers, she overheard a classmate describe her as dumb. She decided to change. In high school, she got straight As, but she had a lot of anxiety. When Beth was sixteen, she became terribly depressed and in her words, "suffered silently."

Despite her challenges, Beth got her master's degree in English and went on to become an English teacher. She eventually earned her doctoral degree at Georgia State University. Graduate work in psychology was challenging, but Beth was able to succeed because of help from a therapist and the supportive environment at Georgia State. She made friends and discovered what she really wanted to do: counsel people one-on-one.

Beth takes Ritalin every day and says it helps her to focus. She's able to focus at work so she can effectively help people in private therapy sessions. Beth says she wouldn't enjoy conducting group therapy sessions because she doesn't do as well with groups as she does with individuals.

When asked what advice she has for young people with ADHD, she says, "Don't be afraid to get all the help you can. Talk to ADHD specialists and find out where support is available. Get evaluated by *an expert. Also know that many kids and adults with ADHD also suffer from depression, anxiety, and loneliness as a result of the frustration of living with undiagnosed ADHD. If that is the case, they really should have psychotherapy as well as medication."*

ADHD is one of the most commonly diagnosed disorders of childhood. There has also been an increase in the number of cases reported in adults in recent years. While public awareness of the disorder is helpful in gaining attention for needed research, there is a lot of incorrect and misleading information available about causes and treatments. Researchers are working hard to sort out the facts through surveys and clinical trials. A clinical trial is a research study created by a government organization (such as the National Institutes of Health in the United States), hospital, or other professional group to find out how treatments work.

USA TODAY Snapshots®

Kids' learning and attention disorders

In 2002, nearly 5 million children between 3 and 17 had a learning disability and about 4.4 million had Attention Deficit Hyperactivity Disorders (ADHD).

Boys vs. girls with ADHD:

BOYS 10%

Girls

4%

Source: National Centers for Health Statistics' estimates; (March 2004 press release)

By Shannon Reilly and Alejandro Gonzalez, USA TODAY, 2004

RECENT DISCOVERIES

Results of a study funded by the National Institute of Mental Health (NIMH) confirmed that children with ADHD do best when they are treated with both medications and behavioral therapy. These children had more relief from their symptoms, better relationships with their parents, and better social skills in general. A follow-up study eight years later showed that more than 60 percent of the kids were able to stop taking medication.

Researchers concluded that treatment should be evaluated regularly. Also, they found that the benefits of the therapy wear off when it is stopped. More research is needed to find effective long-lasting treatments.

Many other studies confirm that combined treatment is the best approach. Other benefits of combined treatment include more effective and positive parenting, normalized behavior in children with ADHD, and a need for lower doses of medication.

DRIVING ACCIDENTS AND ADHD

Inattention behind the wheel is a growing problem. More and more accidents happen while people talk on cell phones, text, eat, or drink.

People with ADHD should limit distractions while driving. Researchers have found that drivers with ADHD are much more likely to be at fault in accidents than those without ADHD.

While almost everyone is guilty of not paying attention while driving 100 percent of the time, for young people with ADHD, the problem is a lot bigger.

According to Daniel Cox, a researcher at the University of Virginia, drivers with ADHD are four times more likely to be at fault in car accidents, three times more likely to have serious injuries, and eight times more likely to have their drivers' licenses suspended than non-ADHD drivers. They are also more likely to back up without looking or run into a stopped car.

Cox's study found that many young people with ADHD who drive do so without taking their ADHD medications. Cox says medications were shown to improve the driving of people with ADHD in laboratory tests.

ADHD AND WORKING MEMORY

Working memory is a problem for people with ADHD. Working memory is an executive function of the brain that enables it to temporarily store and manage information to carry out complex mental tasks, like reading comprehension and solving math problems.

In one study of working memory, children used a computer training program called Cogmed Working Memory Training. The study found that working memory in children with ADHD was improved more by the training than by stimulant medications.

Scientists used to think that working memory couldn't be changed. But recent research shows that working memory can be expanded through focused training.

HYPERACTIVITY AND ALERTNESS

Psychology professor Mark D. Rapport at the University of Central Florida investigated hyperactivity in children with ADHD. He found that children with ADHD are more alert when they are doing things

July 1, 2009

From the Pages of USA TODAY

Medical panel pinpoints 100 areas to examine

A report lists the top 100 areas of medicine in which research is needed to determine which treatments or preventive measures work best.

The federal stimulus package contained $400 million for "comparativeness effectiveness research"—head-to-head comparisons designed to identify which services work best for which individuals. The goal is to ensure that the U.S. health care system gets the most value for its dollar while improving Americans' health.

The Department of Health and Human Services asked the Institute of Medicine, created by Congress to provide advice to policymakers, health professionals, the private sector and the public, to identify the top priorities on which to spend the money.

An IOM [Institute of Medicine] committee winnowed down 2,600 nominations from patients, doctors, professional organizations, and payers of health care to the top 100.

Top priorities in the new report range from how best to prevent the elderly from falling to the best way to manage serious emotional disorders in children and adults to eliminating antibiotic-resistant infections in hospitals.

—Rita Rubin

that challenge their brain's ability to hold information for short periods of time. As a result, they move around a lot. Rapport studied eight- to twelve-year-old boys as they manipulated computer-generated letters, numbers, and shapes while wearing special devices to record their movements. The boys with ADHD became much more active, moving their hands and feet and swiveling in their chairs, than others without ADHD during those tasks.

The findings show that teachers and parents should let their children with ADHD fidget, because limiting their physical activity could limit what they can mentally achieve. Teachers and parents can also provide written instructions, simplify multistep directions, and use checklists to make it easier for children with ADHD to learn. The results of the study may also explain how stimulant medications work, by increasing alertness and improving working memory.

THE FUTURE FOR PEOPLE WITH ADHD

ADHD is a complex disorder that isn't easily understood. Doctors, researchers, and other professionals do not always agree on what causes ADHD or how it should be treated. No single therapy works for all people with ADHD. As the stories in this book show, each person's circumstances and individual health histories have an enormous impact on how effectively he or she copes with ADHD.

Long-term outcomes for people with ADHD still depend greatly on how well they are diagnosed, treated, and supported in their family and community. Researchers are making progress in predicting how people with ADHD may benefit from different types of ADHD therapy. Meanwhile, the best thing that people with ADHD, their families, and society in general can do is to be aware of and educated about the disorder. This is important not only in diagnosing and treating ADHD but in helping society to accept people with this and other disorders.

GLOSSARY

accommodations: helpful aids in an educational or work-related setting. These aids can include special equipment, different performance standards, or special classes.

adverse event: a negative event—specifically, a bad reaction to a medication

advocate: someone who supports or promotes the interests of another person or the person's own interests

alternative medicine: a system of healing or treating disease that isn't taught in conventional medical school. Examples include chiropractic (chiropractors manipulate or move certain body parts, such as the spine, to heal disease) and naturopathy (naturopaths use herbs, massage, acupuncture, and other treatments to heal disease).

behavioral disorder: a disorder that affects how a person acts

conduct disorder: a disorder that causes antisocial behavior, such as stealing, bullying, and violating the rights of others

controlled substance: a drug or chemical whose manufacture, possession, and use are regulated by a government. Controlled substances include illegal drugs and prescription medications. Some controlled substances are addictive.

defiant: constantly challenging or fighting with others

dopamine: a neurotransmitter in the brain that is very important to the body's nervous system

executive functions: higher thought processes in the brain that help a person plan and solve problems. They also help people learn from the past, think before they make decisions, and reach goals.

hyperactive: overly active

impairment: something that causes a physical or mental weakness

impulsive: tending to do things without thinking about them first

inattentive: not paying attention

integrative therapy: therapy that combines regular and alternative medicine

intervention: an action or tool that can help with a difficult task or behavior. Examples include reminder charts that help people with ADHD remember tasks and support groups that help people with ADHD to cope and feel less alone.

learning disorder: a disorder in a person of normal intelligence that causes difficulty learning a specific skill, such as writing, or a specific subject, such as math or reading

neurofeedback: a therapy that uses monitoring instruments to measure and feed back information about brain activity

neurologist: a doctor or scientist who studies or treats disorders of the nervous system

norepinephrine: a neurotransmitter and a hormone similar to adrenaline

oppositional defiant disorder: a behavior disorder marked by continually fighting against authority figures, disobeying them beyond what is considered to be normal, arguing too much with others, annoying others on purpose, and blaming others for one's own mistakes

pediatrician: a doctor who diagnoses and treats infants, children, adolescents, teens, and sometimes young adults

pervasive developmental disorders (PDD): a group of conditions that involve delays in the development of many basic skills, especially the ability to socialize with others, communicate, and use imagination. Children with these conditions are often confused in their thinking and generally have problems understanding the world around them.

psychiatrist: a doctor who diagnoses and treats mental disorders. A psychiatrist can also prescribe medications and provide counseling to a person with a mental illness.

psychologist: a doctor who diagnoses and treats mental disorders. Psychologists provide counseling to people with mental disorders to increase their self-esteem and help them to cope. A psychologist cannot prescribe medications.

sensory integrative dysfunction disorder (SID): a disorder that involves difficulty processing information from the five senses (sight, touch, hearing, taste, and smell)

stimulants: drugs that temporarily increase mental or physical function. Stimulant medications raise the level of dopamine, a chemical in the brain that helps movement, behavior, and attention.

tic: a movement a person can't control

working memory: the brain's ability to hold and work with information for short periods of time

RESOURCES

ADDitude
39 West 37th Street, 15th Floor
New York, NY 10018
http://www.additudemag.com

This periodical provides information, resources, and stories for people with ADHD and their loved ones.

ADHD Aware
P.O. Box 459
Doylestown, PA 18901
http://www.adhdaware.org

This nonprofit organization is run by and for people with ADHD. It supports, advocates, and serves children, adults, and families through programs directed at diverse populations affected by ADHD. ADHD Aware also strives to increase public awareness and understanding of ADHD.

American Academy of Child and Adolescent Psychiatry
3615 Wisconsin Avenue NW
Washington, DC 20016-3007
202-966-7300
http://www.aacap.org

AACAP is a nonprofit organization composed of more than seventy-five hundred child and adolescent psychiatrists and other interested physicians who actively research, evaluate, diagnose, and treat psychiatric disorders in American children and adolescents.

American Academy of Pediatrics
141 Northwest Point Boulevard
Elk Grove Village, IL 60007-1098
847-434-4000
http://www.aap.org

AAP is an organization of pediatricians dedicated to the physical, mental, and social health and well-being of all infants, children, adolescents, and young adults.

American Psychiatric Association
1000 Wilson Boulevard
Suite 1825
Arlington, VA 22209
888-35-PSYCH (888-357-7924)

http://www.psych.org

This medical specialty society has more than thirty-eight thousand international member physicians who work together to ensure humane care and effective treatment for people with mental disorders.

American Psychological Association
750 First Street NE
Washington, DC 20002-4242
800-374-2721, or 202-336-5500
http://www.apa.org

APA is a scientific and professional organization that represents psychology in the United States. It is the largest association of psychologists worldwide.

Attention Deficit Disorder Association
P.O. Box 7557
Wilmington, DE 19803-9997
800-939-1019
http://www.add.org

This international nonprofit organization offers information, resources, and networking opportunities for adults with ADHD.

Centers for Disease Control and Prevention
1600 Clifton Road
Atlanta, GA 30333
800-CDC-INFO (800-232-4636), or 888-232-6348
http://www.cdc.gov

A government agency (part of the U.S. Department of Health and Human Services), CDC is designed to protect the health of all people; prevent disease, injury, and disability; and prepare for new health threats.

Children and Adults with Attention Deficit/Hyperactivity Disorder (CHADD)
8181 Professional Place, Suite 150
Landover, MD 20785
301-306-7070
http://www.chadd.org

This national nonprofit organization provides education, advocacy, and support for children and adults with ADHD. Among other programs, the organization has a Parent to Parent program for parents who are learning how to cope with a child with ADHD.

National Institute of Mental Health
6001 Executive Boulevard, Room 8184, MSC 9663
Bethesda, MD 20892-9663
301-443-4513, or 866-615-6464
http://www.nimh.nih.gov

NIMH is a governmental organization for the prevention, recovery, and cure of mental illnesses through internal research and funding the research of scientists across the country.

National Resource Center on ADHD (a program of CHADD)
8181 Professional Place, Suite 150
Landover, MD 20785
800-233-4050
http://help4adhd.org

The resource center is a national clearinghouse for science-based information about ADHD for professionals and the general public. Funding is through a cooperative agreement with the Centers for Disease Control and Prevention.

Summer Treatment Program at the Center for Children and Families at the State University of New York at Buffalo
106 Diefendorf Hall
3435 Main Street
Buffalo, NY 14214
716-829-2244
http://ccf.buffalo.edu/STP.php

This program offers an ADHD treatment program to address children's behavioral, emotional, and learning problems.

World Health Organization (WHO)
Avenue Appia 20
1211 Geneva 27
Switzerland
+41 22 791 21 11
http://www.who.int/en/

WHO, part of the United Nations, provides leadership and direction on health issues, research, and policies throughout the world.

SELECTED BIBLIOGRAPHY

American Psychiatric Association. *Diagnostic and Statistical Manual of Mental Disorders*. 4th ed. Arlington, VA: 2000.

Barklay, Russell A. *Attention Deficit Hyperactivity Disorder: A Handbook for Diagnosis and Treatment*. New York: Guilford Press, 1990.

Bock, Kenneth, and Cameron Stauth. *Healing the New Childhood Epidemics: Autism, ADHD, Asthma, and Allergies*. New York: Ballantine Books, 2007.

Edge Foundation. "How a Coach Helps." Edgefoundation.org. 2010. http://www.edgefoundation.org/parents/how-a-coach-helps/ (November 3, 2009).

Greenspan, Stanley I. *Overcoming ADHD*. Philadelphia: Da Capo Press, 2009.

Hoffmann, Heinrich. *Slovenly Peter (or Pretty Stories and Funny Pictures for Little Children)*. 1844. Reprint. Rutland, VT: Charles E. Tuttle Company, 1969.

McCarthy Flynn, Laura. "Your ADHD Diagnosis: How to Make Sure It's Accurate." Additudemag.com. N.d. http://www.additudemag.com/adhd/article/6168-5.html (October 14, 2009).

National Institutes of Health. *Attention Deficit Hyperactivity Disorder*. Nimh.nih.gov. N.d. http://www.nimh.nih.gov/health/publications/attention-deficit-hyperactivity-disorder/index.shtml (February 7, 2010).

National Resource Center on AD/HD. "Educational Rights for Children with AD/HD in Public Schools (WWK4)." 2007. http://www.help4adhd.org/en/education/rights/WWK4 (November 5, 2009).

———. "IDEA (The Individual with Disabilities Education Act)." Help4adhd.org. N.d. http://www.help4adhd.org/en/education/rights/idea (September 9, 2009).

Shapiro, Lawrence. *An Ounce of Prevention: How Parents Can Stop Childhood Behavioral and Emotional Problems before They Start*. New York: HarperCollins Publishers, 2000.

U.S. Department of Education. "Special Education and Rehabilitative Services: Children with ADD/ADHD—Topic Brief." ED.gov. July 19, 2007. http://www.ed.gov/policy/speced/leg/idea/brief6.html (September 9, 2009).

U.S. Department of Justice. "Americans with Disabilities Act of 1990, as Amended." Ada.gov. N.d. http://www.ada.gov/pubs/adastatute08.htm (October 21, 2009).

U.S. Food and Drug Administration, "Risks for ADHD Drugs Outlined in Patient Guides." Fda.gov. April 23, 2007. http://www.fda.gov/ForConsumers/ConsumerUpdates/ucm107863.htm (September 4, 2009).

FURTHER READING AND WEBSITES

Books

Davis, Leslie, Harvey Parker, and Sandi Sirotowitz. *Study Strategies Made Easy: A Practical Plan for School Success*. Plantation, FL: Specialty Press, 1996.

Gantos, Jack. *Joey Pigza Swallowed the Key*. New York: HarperCollins, 2000. This novel is told from the point of view of Joey Pigza, a boy in grade school dealing with ADHD.

Hyman, Bruce M., Ph.D., and Cherry Pedrick, R.N. *Obsessive-Compulsive Disorder*. Rev. ed. Minneapolis: Twenty-First Century Books, 2009.

Martin, Kirk. *Gifted: A Novel*. HIgh Point, NC: Cantwell-Hamilton Press, 2005. This is a story of a high school student with ADHD trying to find out where he fits into the high school social network.

Moragne, Wendy. *Depression*. Minneapolis: Twenty-First Century Books, 2001.

Robin, Arthur L. *ADHD in Adolescents: Diagnosis and Treatment*. New York: Guilford Press, 1998.

Rodriguez, Ana Maria. *Autism and Asperger Syndrome*. Minneapolis: Twenty-First Century Books, 2009.

Taylor, Blake E. S. *ADHD & Me: What I Learned from Lighting Fires at the Dinner Table*. Oakland: New Harbinger Publications, 2007.

Vincent, Annick. *My Brain Needs Glasses: Living With Hyperactivity*. Lac-Beuport, Canada: Academie Impact, 2005.

Walker, Beth. *Girl's Guide to AD/HD: Don't Lose This Book!* Bethesda, MD: Woodbine House, 2004.

Wilens, Timothy. *Straight Talk About Psychiatric Medication For Kids*. 3rd edition. New York: Guilford Press, 2008.

Websites

Attention Deficit Disorder Resources
http://w3.addresources.org/
This is the website of ADD Resources, a nonprofit organization that provides resources, support, and networking opportunities for children and adults with ADHD and ADD.

Centers for Disease Control and Prevention—Attention-Deficit/Hyperactivity Disorder (ADHD)
http://www.cdc.gov/ncbddd/adhd/conditions.html
This government site provides users with reliable information on ADHD.

National Mental Health Information Center—Mental Health Services Locator
http://mentalhealth.samhsa.gov/databases/
This locator, created by the U.S. Department of Health and Human Services' Substance Abuse and Mental Health Services Administration, provides comprehensive information about mental health services and resources for professionals, consumers and their families, and the general public. Visitors to the site can access information by selecting a state or U.S. territory from the map or drop-down menu.

Nemours Foundation—ADHD
http://kidshealth.org/teen/diseases_conditions/learning/adhd.html
This site, run by the nonprofit Nemours Center for Children's Health Media, provides accurate and timely information about ADHD and other health issues. The content is directed at teens and is related in a straightforward manner.

Technical Assistance Alliance for Parent Centers (the ALLIANCE)
http://www.taalliance.org/about/index.asp
The ALLIANCE is funded by the U.S. Department of Education's Office of Special Education Programs (OSEP). It is one of seven projects that coordinate more than 100 parent training and information centers and community parent resource centers under the Individuals with Disabilities Education Act. Visitors to this website who type in "ADHD" will find a wide range of information for parents of children with ADHD.

U.S. Department of Education and the American Institutes for Research—
Identifying and Treating Attention Deficit Hyperactivity Disorder: A Resource for School and Home
http://www2.ed.gov/teachers/needs/speced/adhd/adhd-resource-pt1.pdf
This report, written by the U.S. Department of Education and the American Institutes for Research, offers a comprehensive look at ADHD in the school setting, including the legal requirements for identifying and providing educational services to children with ADHD, as well as treatment options and tips for improving performance in school.

INDEX

ABOUT THE AUTHOR

Amy Farrar has been in business for herself as a freelance writer and editor since 1999 and has worked in the publishing field for more than twenty years. She is the author of *Global Warming* (Essential Viewpoints) and *The Indispensable Field Guide to Freelance Writing*. Amy lives in Minnesota with her husband, Paul, her daughter, Emma, and their two cats.

PHOTO ACKNOWLEDGMENTS

The images in this book are used with the permission of: © Gregor Schuster/CORBIS, pp. 1, 3; © White Packert/Iconica/Getty Images, p. 7; © Jetta Productions/Stone/ Getty Images, p. 8; © Mary Evans Picture Library/The Image Works, pp. 11, 12; © Sean Justice/Photonica/Getty Images, p. 18; © ColorBlind Images/Iconica/Getty Images, p. 21; © Steve Liss/Time & Life Pictures/Getty Images, p. 22; © Buccina Studios/Photodisc/Getty Images, p. 23; © Patricia McDonough/CORBIS, p. 24; Brookhaven National Laboratory, p. 30; Custom Medical Stock Photo, pp. 32, 49 (right); © Jac Depczyk/Photographer's Choice/Getty Images, p. 33; © SW Productions/Photodisc/Getty Images, p. 34; © PhotoAlto/Ale Ventura/Getty Images, p. 38; © Patti Sapone/Star Ledger/CORBIS, p. 40; © Ariel Skelley/Blend Images/ Getty Images, p. 43; © john angerson/Alamy, p. 49 (left); © VOISIN/PHANIE/Photo Researchers, Inc., p. 58; © Jupiterimages/Comstock Images/Getty Images, p. 60; © Ravl/Dreamstime.com, p. 66; © David McNew/Getty Images, p. 68; Library of Congress, pp. 76 (left, LC-USZ62-41756), 76 (right, LC-USZC4-4940); © Brendan Smialowski/Getty Images, p. 77; © Fotosearch/Archive Photos/Getty Images, p. 85; © Stretch Photography/Blend Images/Getty Images, p. 87; © Eileen Blass/ USA TODAY, p. 93; © Ned Frisk/Blend Images/Getty Images, p. 96.

Cover: © iStockphoto.com/Andrey Prokhorov (EKG); © Gregor Schuster/CORBIS (MRI scan of brain).